Tales From the Sunroom

An Anthology of Inspirational Short Stories

Gail Cauble Gurley

Tales From the Sunroom is a work of fiction. Any references to actual people, events, establishments, organizations, or locales are intended only to give the fiction a sense of reality and authenticity. Other names, characters, places, and incidents portrayed herein are either the product of the author's imagination or are used fictionally.

Tales From the Sunroom. Copyright © 2001 by Gail Cauble Gurley. All rights reserved. Printed in the United States of America. No part of this book may be reproduced or reused in any manner whatsoever without written permission except in the case of brief quotations embodied in critical articles and reviews.

For ordering or other information, write:
Cottage Garden Publishing
P. O. Box 5641
High Point, NC 27262
E-mail: cottagegardenpub@cs.com
Website: www.CottageGardenPublishing.com

"The Message" from *Storied Crossings* used with permission of Scribes Hill Publishing and David Repsher, Publisher.

FIRST EDITION

Library of Congress Control Number: 2001118453

ISBN 0-9713316-0-X

First Printing: October 2001

10 09 08 07 06 05 04 03 02 01

In loving memory of my parents Grayson and Vera Lingle Cauble; my grandmother Minnie F. Lingle; and James Ray Hill. They nurtured and inspired me, believed in me and loved me, even when I wasn't lovable.

With special gratitude and love to Ed, my devoted husband; Denise Barnes, our beautiful daughter; her husband, Tony; and our FANTASTIC grandchildren, Charlie, Spencer and Madison. Thank you all for your patience, pride and confidence in me and my work.
I love you all.

Special thanks to my good friend and a very gifted young man, Jeff Pate, best-selling author of *Winner Take All* and *Eye of the Beholder* for his expert advice, unselfish encouragement and professional support. His gracious help in creating this work was invaluable.

CONTENTS

	Preface	vi
1	The Message	1
2	Come the Spring	13
3	The Gray Lady	25
4	The Guide	37
5	The Transient	47
6	Toby and Beau	65
7	Daughter of the Mountain	77
8	Connected	87
9	Beyond the Gossamer Veil	111
10	The Gazebo	127

Preface

One cold, winter morning, my husband and I sat in the church we attend when our minister issued a challenge. He challenged all in the congregation to offer any glory we receive or success we attain to God, as He is the source from which all good arrives. It was at that precise moment that I made the decision to fulfill a lifelong ambition to write. Other than a few published poems and an article in an academic journal while in college, I never found the time or courage to dedicate my efforts to this craft. It was now or never.

I entered a short story writing contest, was one of the winners with my story "The Message" and had my story accepted for publication in *Storied Crossings* by Scribes Hill Publishing in Salem, Virginia.

These tales originated in the sunroom of my home with inspiration from the sun, rain, birds, squirrels, flowers and our pet dog Molly playing in our fenced-in backyard. These scenes recalled childhood memories as well as produced ideas from my heart. The words are directly from heaven, and I'm pleased to have been the channel for their conversion.

My youth was blessed by the presence of loving unselfish people. All that my parents gave to my sister and me was all that they had. My grandmother was equally unselfish. She was monetarily poor but exceedingly wealthy in generosity and kindness. She was a revered guide.

It was only after leaving the beloved refuge of my early home that I discovered selfishness, greed and ugliness. It was a difficult lesson from which no one could protect me, or any other child of our world, as we must all share the heritage of this hard, seemingly cruel education. Adversity, however, builds strength and character—strength to survive life's difficulties, and character to muster the integrity not to become corrupted.

The world can be, and is, a beautiful and loving place in spite of the negative factions abounding. I have attempted to identify in my work the resilience and recuperative power of the human spirit. We can experience physical pain, emotional pain, loss, tragedy, anger or rejection, and emerge largely unscathed due to the innate gift of faith and hope as well as the will to survive. That is an endowment unsurpassed by any force within our world and can only be identified as otherworldly and divine in origin.

There are too many wonderful people in my life who give their love and support unconditionally for me to name them all individually. But special gratitude goes to my family; Jeff Pate, a gifted author; Randy Delling for his expert help with that mysterious machine, the computer; and my dear friend, Jeanette Shirley, my book cover designer. Without their help and confidence, I could never have realized my dream to write.

There are messages for all who travel into my literary world of soothing, inspiring adventures. Enjoy your journey through the dimensions of my stories!

To God be the glory!

The Message

What we love is always near. It rests in our hearts, our minds, our memories.

—g. gurley

Jodie ran across the end of the expansive front porch, easing by the large porch swing suspended from the ceiling where she spent so many happy hours on her visits, crossed the remaining space and burst through the front door. She skipped over the wool living room rug, worn thin from the entrance to the opposite door by countless feet and numerous decades.

As she entered the front door, which was never locked, she shouted eagerly, "Grandmother!"

"Yo," came her grandmother's reply from the kitchen.

Jodie rushed down the hall of what was once the dining room to reach her grandmother in the kitchen. When Amanda Poole's sons had returned from World War II, they had closed up a large portion of the existing dining room and installed a bathroom so as to update the large home. Jodie didn't remember when it was a dining room but she did remember going outside to the bathroom. This new room had been a welcomed addition.

She finally reached the warm embrace of her grandmother and snuggled comfortably against the familiar texture of her

TALES FROM THE SUNROOM

worn, cotton apron. Her aprons had bibs which slipped over her head and sashes tied sassily at the waist. They were created by Amanda and included pockets trimmed with bright rick rack. Jodie always encountered the familiar apron when she entered the house. Even on Sunday mornings before church, the apron would be tied securely over special dresses or suits until time to depart. It would be removed and hooked over a nail by the door as Amanda left the house, to be retrieved as soon as she returned from church several hours later.

Jodie's mother and younger sister made a more dignified entry behind her and arrived to an equally warm welcome. Jodie treasured her time with her grandmother and would always strive to arrive first so as to receive the first generous hug.

Margaret and 6-year-old Lynn left Jodie there while they went to the doctor for Lynn's pre-school physical examination and vaccinations before Lynn entered first grade. School started in four weeks so Jodie's visits were particularly precious now.

She slipped quietly into the hallowed pantry which was attached to the back of the kitchen. Jodie felt that she was entering a special, almost holy place when she descended the five wooden steps into the small dark room. One tiny window at the west end of the room allowed the sun to cut through the dusty interior in long, smoky ropes. Jodie loved to brush her hand through the sun and watch the dust specks scamper and flutter about. These sun ropes would travel across the room throughout the afternoon, illuminating the treasures stored on the groaning shelves of bounty. Amanda tended a large vegetable garden and various fruit trees each year, and worked tirelessly to preserve these crops for the winter. Her philosophy was "Waste not, want not."

The sun was slicing over the delicious sweetness of preserves and jellies which were Jodie's favorites among the plenty. The

The Message

plums sparkled like royal amethysts under the golden beam while the apple jelly broadcast a bright, warm crimson, promising a sweet, delectable future treat. The strawberry was clouded with seeds but these tiny spots twinkled like stars under the sun's intrusion. Her favorite among the bounty, however, was the thick, ebony, sinfully rich blackberry jelly. When the rays reached these special treasures, the darkness in the jars resembled luxurious, opulent black velvet, and Jodie's heart would soar and her mouth water at the memory of the decadent richness inside.

Just beyond the jars of delectable fruits set the practical, sturdy offerings of canned vegetables. Corn, tomatoes, green beans, pickles and okra stood proudly, packed with vitamins and minerals and good health. Jodie scrunched up her nose slightly as the sun slipped across these essentials. The yellows, versatile greens and even rich reds were no match for the jewel tones of the fruited elixir of the jellies and preserves. She knew they were good for her and were necessary to consume in order to reach the ecstasy of the sweet jars, but they were merely an unpleasantness she had to endure. The rule was no dessert until all her vegetables had been eaten.

She loved to follow Amanda around the large kitchen as fruits and vegetables, which the two of them had gathered from the yard and garden, were washed and prepared for immediate consumption or future enjoyment. Amanda would sit on a stool by the kitchen window and snap, shell or peel while Jodie leaned against her elbow, watching every move and helping when she could.

Amanda was a petite woman in her mid-60s with gray hair tied up in a neat bun resting on her neck. When she let it down to brush, it fell below her waist. She wore no makeup and never had. She had beautiful blue eyes which glittered with mirth and intelligence. Her hands and feet were twisted by arthritis but no one had ever heard her complain. It slowed her down a bit but certainly did not stop her. She wore long, practical dresses of faded cotton, dimmed by numerous washings as well as the hot North Carolina sun as they hung on the backyard clothesline to dry.

Her shoes were sensible black leather, low topped so as not to cause discomfort to her twisted ankles, and were tied with a simple black shoestring. She wore stockings rolled down below her knees in order not to hinder her bending and stooping as she worked, but they were never visible as her dress reached below her shins.

Jodie was enthralled by the shoes. When Amanda removed them, they retained the form of her misshapen feet, and Jodie would run her fingers over the lumps, bumps and occasional cut put there with a razor blade to allow swollen tissue to stretch.

She was petite like her grandmother with the same large blue eyes. In addition to the intelligence emanating, there was a maturity and wisdom present which went well beyond Jodie's eight years. She soaked up everything her grandmother said, and like her grandmother, loved to read. She had a voracious appetite for books and frequently had her "nose in one," as Grandmother would remark. Amanda had instilled a love of knowledge in all seven of her children as well as her twenty-one grandchildren.

Amanda and her late husband Tom had both gone to college. This was a very rare occurrence in 1906 America, especially for a woman. Amanda wanted to be a teacher and Tom dreamed of being an architect.

Two years into her education, Amanda's father died and she was forced to leave college. A year later, Tom's father died and he too left behind his dreams of being an architect. He became a carpenter, building strong, sturdy homes and built a small one to share with Amanda after their marriage. Shortly afterwards,

The Message

the babies started coming, and Amanda stayed at home to care for them. She never regretted her fate, however, and thrived in the role of wife, homemaker and mother as well as sometime music teacher on the pump organ in the front room. These lessons brought in much needed nickels and dimes in lean times. She was equally successful as a grandmother and was deeply revered by her grandchildren.

The tiny house was expanded through the years as the family grew. Jodie had always known that rooms were added to the house and would frequently lie on the floor studying the ceilings and floors, trying to determine how the additions were joined. Tom was such an expert craftsman that it was extremely difficult to determine exactly where these add-ons occurred. He had died in 1937, so Jodie had never known him since she had not yet been born, but studying the workmanship on the walls helped her feel close to his memory. He seemed to be alive in those very walls he had so lovingly crafted.

Jodie left the deliciousness of the pantry to seek out her grandmother. "Grandmother," she called out.

"I'm in the yard, Jodie," Amanda called back.

Jodie shoved the back screen door open, slamming it against the wall, bounded down the twelve wooden steps off the back porch, and rushed to her grandmother's side. She was on her knees at the flowerbed, digging into the rich earth and retrieving tiny flower bulbs.

Jodie was enchanted by her grandmother's flowerbed. There were numerous species and colors and aromas present throughout the year. Amanda was digging in the jonquil bed.

"What are you doing to the jonquils?" Jodie inquired.

"Thinning them out and moving some of the bulbs to another area."

"Why?"

TALES FROM THE SUNROOM

"Because they're too thick and unless I thin them out, they won't bloom as well next spring." Amanda was amused by Jodie's curiosity. She sounded almost defensive of the bulbs. She was glad that Jodie loved her home so much. It validated Amanda's and Tom's presence and purpose on earth.

Jodie moved away from the jonquil bed to explore other areas of the yard. It was not a large yard but was well planned and amply planted. In addition to the large umbrella shade tree which was the focal point, there was a large apple tree, a mature lilac bush, and a huge fig bush which grew up the side of the house and nestled under the kitchen window. The apples and lilacs were gone for this year, but the figs were hard, green obelisks, waiting to ripen and release their sweet brown goodness.

Jodie's eyes rested on the mass of burgundy daisy mums just beginning to burst open among the iris leaves, which stood guard at the property line beside the house next door. She loved to kneel among these rich jewels and rub her hands, arms, and face over their thickness. The pungent odor was not as pleasant as the butter yellow jonquils, but was hardy, substantial, and earthy. She enjoyed weaving them together to make a regal crown for her head, and she knew that Grandmother would never scold her for breaking them off. She was careful not to pull the plants up by the root and only picked what she needed to make her crown or fill a vase.

"Why aren't any of these yellow, Grandmother?"

Amanda was caught off guard by the question but wasn't surprised. Yellow was Jodie's favorite color, and she would frequently bring into the house collections of various yellow flowers including wild buttercups, the happy jonquils, and even dandelions peeking up through the grass.

"Well, they aren't yellow because they're red, Jodie." Amanda struggled for an answer. "They've always been that color."

The Message

"Will they ever be yellow?"

"I don't think so, honey. The message to be red is in their roots and genes, and they'll forever be that way." Jodie was disappointed but accepted the explanation and made no further mention of it.

Sundays were particularly pleasant for Jodie. After attending the Lutheran church in their small village of Charity, the whole family would meet at Amanda's house for lunch. Everyone would bring food and the long kitchen table would bow under the load of deliciousness set before the noisy, laughing crowd. Jodie would eat until she was near bursting.

The women would clean up while the men retreated to the comfortable, worn living room. The young would escape outside during the summer and into the front bedroom in cold weather. There were huge chests and an armoire in Amanda's room to hide in, and tall beds and thick-legged tables to hide under. Frequently, there would be a quilt frame set up with a quilt in progress, and it encompassed most of the room so they would play endless games of cowboys and Indians in teepees, or become kings and queens living in a castle, or cavemen living in caves.

The years sped by and Jodie grew up as Amanda grew older. Jodie's love for her grandmother and all the treasured memories and activities at her home, however, did not diminish. She felt no embarrassment because of her love for her grandmother, nor did she consider that love unsophisticated, as did many of her more worldly peers.

As Amanda advanced in years, she remained busy and active, continuing to raise her garden, can her vegetables and make the delightful fruit preserves and jellies. She thrived on the continued love and devotion from her family, especially her grandchildren.

Jodie graduated high school and college, married and moved

an hour away from her beloved grandmother; however, she managed to visit her each weekend. She never left Amanda's home without a gift, and after they moved into their new home, Amanda would present various bulbs and plants she had dug out of the yard. Jodie would rush home and place them in a carefully prepared spot of honor in the yard. Soon the small yard was filled with botanical offerings and became a miniature replica of Amanda's yard.

Each spring, Jodie would watch with eager anticipation until the first jonquils burst forth in their yellow beauty. Sometimes they bloomed in a late winter snow, and were always the first on the block to appear. The vintage flowers were more fragrant than the scientifically engineered ones from new bulbs at other homes on the block. Jodie's blossoms were smaller but would light up a room with their glory and fragrance.

The long awaited burgundy daisy mums would bloom in the fall, and each year they became thicker as the roots spread with proliferation. They were set in the upper corner of the backyard and cascaded regally down the hill. Jodie would sit below them in the warmth of the early fall sunshine, basking in their beauty and running her fingers through the buds. She enjoyed picking and weaving crowns for herself and her daughter, Mandy, Amanda's namesake. Like Jodie, Mandy spent many happy hours at the home of her great-grandmother, learning and laughing and loving.

In the year of her 90th birthday, Amanda began to fade. Jodie and Mandy made an effort to visit with her each weekend. The vegetable garden had long ago been abandoned and the beloved flowerbeds were matted with weeds and overgrowth. The succulent sweetness of the jellies and preserves was no more than a pleasant memory. Jodie and Mandy would dig in the dirt to remove weeds and thin out flowers choked by their own propagation.

The Message

Amanda watched the two working as she sat sadly in a chair. She longed to sink her fingers into the warm, moist earth and smell the rich, dark fertility she had worked in for so many years. She could see the tangles of roots and the occasional earthworm wriggling about, keeping the earth from becoming packed and adding food to the plants.

Jodie and Mandy were aware of her painful silence, and maintained a light and cheerful bantering as they worked. Jodie scooped up a double handful of the dirt and placed it gently in the lap of Amanda's apron. Her blue eyes, clouded by cataracts and age, sparkled with tears, love, and gratitude as she smiled warmly at Jodie. She pressed her hands into the soil and lifted it to her nose. She could not only smell the musty darkness but she could taste the richness. It was more delicious than any meal she had ever consumed.

In the late summer, Amanda suffered a massive cerebral hemorrhage. She managed to reach Margaret by telephone and ask for help. Margaret rushed to her after calling an ambulance, and accompanied her mother to the hospital. Later that evening after Amanda had stabilized, she called Jodie.

Jodie's heart lurched when she received the news from her mother, and she felt panicky, even after being assured that Amanda was resting comfortably. She knew without being told that this was the beginning of the end for her beloved grandmother.

Several weeks later, Amanda was moved into a nursing home. Jodie and Mandy continued their weekly visits, and Jodie would sit by Amanda's bed, reading the church bulletin to her, showing her family photographs and just holding her hand. Each time they left, Amanda would plead with them to take her home. Jodie felt helpless, standing on the edge of effectiveness, viewing the situation without hope.

TALES FROM THE SUNROOM

The treasured burgundy daisy mums bloomed right on schedule that late September, and she gathered huge masses of them to place in Amanda's room. Amanda was getting weaker but she always recognized them and managed a smile when Jodie or Mandy entered. She eventually became too weak to speak but managed to raise her hand to touch them with a greeting of welcome.

In early November with the season's final bouquet of Jodie's mums by her bedside, Amanda Poole quietly slipped away.

Jodie was in deep despair, moving numbly through the funeral and the days and weeks following. She knew that her life would never again be the same. She had not only lost her beloved grandmother, her friend and mentor, but she had lost her childlike innocence regarding life. She had never before lost a loved one and even though she certainly knew what death was, it had never struck so close to her heart before.

Winter passed and spring arrived. The jonquils exploded, their yellow crowns bobbing happily in the not yet warm sun of the North Carolina March. Jodie placed them on Amanda's grave, weeping quietly and sadly. She was unable to shake this emptiness reaching into the very cellars of her heart and soul.

The summer sweltered that year and Jodie couldn't bring herself to work in the mums. She knew they needed to be weeded but the grief, not the heat, kept her away from that corner.

Summer waned and early fall arrived. The leaves were particularly beautiful that year. The trees were adorned with vibrant yellows, reds, purples and oranges in hues that Jodie never remembered seeing before. Autumn had always been Jodie's favorite season, and frequently as she was driving home from work that year, she would be so overcome with the breathtaking glory of the colors that she would pull off the street, step outside the car and just soak in the majesty of it all. More than once she

The Message

thought, I wish Grandmother could see this.

October was speeding by and still Jodie procrastinated against approaching the mums. One bright, unusually warm Saturday afternoon common to fall in the south, she moved slowly up the concrete driveway beside her home, past the clothesline, and found herself being pulled across the backyard toward the daisy mum garden.

As she neared the site, she stopped, frozen in place. She gasped in disbelief as she viewed the profusion of blooms. Never had she seen them so thick and lush, but that wasn't what took her breath away. The familiar dark burgundy flowed across the patch but about three quarters of the way through, the burgundy began to fade and lighten to paler amber, beige and another breathtakingly unexplainable color. As the garden ended, the blooms were no longer burgundy but had gradually become a beautiful, clear golden yellow which was pure in its clarity. There was no hint of burgundy, amber or beige contaminating these beautiful mums.

Jodie cried out in joy, disbelief and sheer ecstasy as she felt the bonds of grief burst and fall away from her heart. Grandmother had sent a loving message that she was fine and still loved Jodie. There was no need to worry or grieve anymore. The feeling of love and compassion in Grandmother's message nearly overwhelmed Jodie, and the tears splashing on these flowers were no longer tears of pain but tears of gratitude and love and relief.

She buried her face in their yellowness and wrapped her fingers around the petals and stems. She slipped a crown of yellow over her red hair and filled her lap with their purity. She filled every vase in her house and loaded masses of them into the car for the trip to the cemetery.

They adorned Grandmother's grave as Jodie thanked her for

sending this special message.

The mums never again bloomed yellow but returned to their original burgundy the following year. That fact only reinforced Jodie's certainty that she had been blessed by this special gift from Grandmother. She was at peace.

Come the Spring

Unlike humans, nature's force joins them to be always as one.

—g. gurley

Joseph stood on the sandy shore with the other stately ganders, strutting and preening so as to impress the smaller, equally stately females bobbing on the serene surface of the tranquil lake. Their cries directed at the floating brood were raucous but pleading as they attempted to catch the eye of the source of their desire.

Joseph's stance was more dignified, albeit anxious, as he had already made his choice. He only hoped that the elegant Elizabeth would accept him. Canada geese mated only once in their lifetime. The mate nature gave them was a lifelong companion, and when one died, the other was alone for the rest of his or her time, so this was no frivolous ceremony.

Elizabeth glided away from the other females, positioning herself nearer the shore where Joseph was holding vigil. He stepped cautiously nearer the water's edge, his head down and neck undulating, his heart filled with hope.

At precisely the same moment, he and Elizabeth caught sight of an object hurling swiftly toward Joseph, wings spread, beak poised with the sharp, teeth-like lamellae lining the surfaces, ready to slice through Joseph's body. It was Buck, a larger, more aggressive male who likewise desired Elizabeth as a mate.

Elizabeth cried out in alarm, Joseph in surprise. The force of Buck's attack coupled with the element of surprise sent Joseph floundering. He struggled valiantly to his feet, and the drama unfolded before the terrified Elizabeth.

Their black beaks and wings gnashed and pounded in their struggle while the white on their under necks flashed as they twisted and tumbled over and over. Joseph was outweighed by the larger Buck but unsurpassed in effort. Joseph had passion, and consequently, more heart, so after a very long, dreadful few minutes, he was victorious over Buck.

Bruised and battered with feathers askew and small droplets of blood splattered on his white neck, he turned wearily but victoriously to Elizabeth. He dropped his head toward the earth and made gentle honking noises to her. She eagerly honked her acceptance of him as her mate, and he moved closer to the water where she waited.

Just as Elizabeth screamed out a warning, he caught sight of an attack from his side. It was Buck. He was refusing to be defeated by the smaller Joseph. As he braced for the attack, Elizabeth left the water, crashing her body into the side of Buck, momentarily stunning and unbalancing him. He regained his composure, turning toward the defiant Elizabeth, but by then Joseph was on him. He quickly evaluated the situation and decided he had had enough. He hastily retreated from the couple and did not return.

Elizabeth approached Joseph anxiously, checking him carefully for injuries. She made soft, soothing sounds, and they both determined his injuries were minor, but he would be sore for a few days. They entered the water together, destined to be side

Come the Spring

by side for the rest of their lives. They were bound together by a special force, mysterious and powerful, pondered by many but understood by none.

They reared their first clutch of five goslings on the shore of the large, upper New York lake that year. Elizabeth constructed the nest of weeds, twigs, grass, moss and pine needles. She heaped them into a mound, rounding out a depression with her body until it was perfectly customized to her shape. This prevented the intrusion of cold air as she incubated the eggs. Even in late April and May, air could be raw coming off the lake. After laying her eggs, she lined the nest with feathers and down from herself and Joseph. This insulated the eggs against both cold and heat, ensuring the possibility of complete and successful hatching.

The first year, Elizabeth noticed that she had built the nest in an area susceptible to strong winds from the lake. She had placed it near a supply of succulent grasses so as to limit her time off the nest for feeding. However, these grasses offered little shelter for her clutch of eggs. Joseph was never far away and would protect it as well as he could – mostly against predators. He was too large to fit on the conformed-to-Elizabeth nest without endangering the eggs, so if the wind became too brisk and Elizabeth was feeding, he would call to her, standing with his wings spread against the gusts until her speedy return. He would then bring her pieces of grass and stems for feeding.

"Joseph, come the spring, I want to build the nest nearer the bank over there," she stated, directing her sight on the gently sloping hill a short distance away. He nodded in agreement.

Each fall, the pair, with various surviving members of their flock which included some of their own offspring, would migrate from upper New York to their wintering grounds in the Louisiana bayous. They soared majestically over New York, Pennsylvania, West Virginia, southwest until reaching the misty, almost ethereal swamps. Elizabeth was particularly fond of flying over the craggy mountains of West Virginia, ablaze with autumn's golds, reds and yellows. She and Joseph would drop below the flock so as to get a better view. Joseph was nervous about this tradition, but he tolerated it since Elizabeth enjoyed it so much.

Joseph and Elizabeth stayed close together during the mild, deep south winter and ventured off their tiny island in the bayou seldom and cautiously. In early and mid-winter, they would hear the frequent rumbling of gunfire. They didn't completely understand what was happening but there seemed to be a connection between the reverberations and the disappearance of flock members. Only in the early dusk after all the sounds of weapons, motorboats and vehicles left the area would they venture out briefly. Elizabeth's natural nervousness and anxiety prescribed this cautious behavior. It was ironic that the beauty of West Virginia's autumn was stronger than her innate cautiousness, while the gunfire alerted all her survival instincts.

She would set on the nest each spring back in New York and create plans for the next season. "Joseph, come the spring..." became an habitual comment. It always related to where and how to place the nest, what materials to use for construction, how to hide the nest from the ever voracious foxes, snakes, hawks and owls. Joseph listened lovingly and patiently, and at the next spring arrival, her plans would be implemented.

At the end of their seventh season on their shoreline, Elizabeth gazed thoughtfully to the shore on the other side of the small bay where they nested.

"Joseph." He braced for the statement as he recognized her tone. "Come the spring, let's build our nest on that shoreline across the bay. I can't believe I haven't thought of it before. There's a steep bank behind it and rocks we can build in to shel-

Come the Spring

ter our babies from the cold and our enemies. It looks like there's plenty of food also so I won't have to go far to eat."

"Yes, Elizabeth. We'll build over there next spring," he replied gently, unable to hide the love and devotion echoing in his voice.

The next morning before dawn, the flock left the lake with frosted beaches and frozen grasses for the annual trek south. Joseph's old rival, Buck, was the leader since he was the largest and strongest but there had been no further confrontations with him. He had mated with the feisty Jessie and had met his match in her high-spirited pride. Joseph sometimes found himself almost pitying Buck's lot in life. Jessie could be a wing-full with her independence and strong will. Buck, however, seemed to thrive on her strength and appeared content. Mother Nature, as always, had done well with her mating declarations, both with Buck and Jessie and Joseph and Elizabeth.

The lake's surface exploded with a host of black wings as the large birds raced across the top for momentum to raise their large bodies into the crisp early pre-dawn. Soon they had formed the familiar V shape of their species, progressing on the air wake of the larger birds in front. This preserved their energy, and they moved slowly so they suffered very little stress throughout the long trip, arriving at their destination healthy and strong.

They approached the West Virginia mountains on their third day out. Elizabeth honked excitedly to Joseph, angled to her right front.

"Joseph, look at the leaves! They're more beautiful than I've ever seen them!"

She dropped out of the formation in her excitement to get closer to the beauty, and Joseph followed her down, uneasy and concerned, but certainly not willing to let her go alone.

Canada geese move slowly through the sky and are so large,

they make ready targets for eager, cunning hunters. The two skulking in the trees couldn't believe their luck as two of these big birds came closer to their hiding place as they left the flock. The thrill coupled with the alcohol caused one of them to stumble, nearly falling. The two beagles with them scampered out of harm's way.

"Careful, stupid!" yelled his companion.

"Don't worry about it," grumbled the clumsy pursuer, retrieving his shotgun which had luckily not discharged when he dropped it.

They recovered enough to get off a couple of shots. One of the birds was hit and plummeted toward the treetops. The dogs burst into exuberant barking, running around with feverish impatience, waiting for the command to go.

"Go!" screamed the men, and all four of the companions, men and dogs alike, crashed through the brush in the general direction of the fallen goose.

There was someone else who heard the shots and saw the wounded goose fall. They also saw the larger goose following behind his injured mate.

Emily and Brandy Johnson were a mother/daughter veterinarian team who loved animals and operated a shelter for injured or abandoned creatures on their sprawling property nestled on the mountainside. Hunting season had not yet legally opened so they were particularly dismayed by the scene. They immediately sprang into action.

"Get the kit," Emily shouted. "I'll get the jeep!"

Brandy bounded out of the house with the first aid kit they used to treat injured animals and leaped into the waiting jeep. They sped off across the fields in the direction of the fateful fall.

The hunters bumbled and stumbled noisily through the brush, trying to locate their quarry. The dogs were confused

Come the Spring

and disoriented by the melee and ran around in circles, barking in frenzy.

Elizabeth fell through the ends of thick branches on a huge oak, breaking her fall and slowing her descent. She landed in a large pile of leaves and pine needles which had been created by a recent strong wind. Joseph landed right behind her calling out in terror, "Elizabeth! Elizabeth!"

She raised her head weakly and whispered, "Joseph, I'm sorry."

He stood there, helplessly enveloped by confusion and anguish. She can't die, he sobbed. She just can't!

He heard dogs barking in the distance and panicked. He looked around desperately, trying to determine a solution.

"Lie very still, Elizabeth, and don't make a sound. I'm going to try to cover you and I'll lead the dogs away but I'll be back. Just hang on! Please!"

"Be careful, my Joseph."

Emily and Brandy arrived at the creek which was full of large rocks and boulders so they had to leave the jeep there. They could hear the dogs approaching their location.

"Take the kit and go on ahead, Brandy. I'll stay here and stop these guys. I'll just bet it's those Martin boys. Probably drunk again too."

"Be careful, Mom," Brandy cautioned as she grabbed the black first aid kit and exited the jeep. She ran across the stream and continued on in the direction of the fallen geese.

In a very short time, the two hunting dogs arrived. She stood in front of them and shouted angrily. They stopped in their tracks, recognizing Emily. They began whimpering and circling. She had always been kind to them but could be stern in her commands. They were reluctant to disobey her order to stop.

"Just as I thought," she retorted to the dogs, "the Martin boys!"

They floundered out of the dense forest and stopped when

TALES FROM THE SUNROOM

they saw her.

"Jeb and Doug, what in blazes are you doing? Have you lost your minds?"

"Aw, shucks, Miss Emily, we're just having fun," Jeb replied sheepishly. They both looked quite uncomfortable under her cold, angry glare.

"You've been warned time and again about hunting before hunting season starts. The sheriff will really be fed up with you this time. Now git! And take your dogs with you!"

They reluctantly turned away, mumbling and grumbling but unwilling to rebuke her confrontation.

"Come on, dogs," they called, and the entire motley gang retreated into the woods.

Emily returned to the jeep, reached into the back seat and retrieved a large canvas bag. She threw it over her shoulder and moved in the same direction Brandy had taken. The bag contained saws, ropes and climbing equipment used in their rescue missions.

Brandy approached the area where she thought the geese had crashed, and as she perused the scene, her eye caught a glimpse of something which didn't fit the terrain. She focused on it and realized it was a Canada goose, lying flat against the ground. Her heart sank as she stepped toward the object. As she approached, he hissed and flapped his wings, moving further away. She followed him for about fifty feet and began to realize that this was a ploy. He was leading her away, probably from his injured mate. It was imperative that she find the missing bird as soon as possible—not only to treat her injuries if she was still alive but to protect her from predators.

She turned away from Joseph and began backtracking. He became very agitated and honked loudly.

Emily arrived on the scene and exclaimed, "I see you've

Come the Spring

found them!"

"Well, just one," she answered. "The male was trying to lead me away so I'm trying to find the female. Did you find out who the hunters were?"

"Yeah, just like I figured."

Brandy shook her head in disgust and anger. "Jerks!" she muttered.

It took ten minutes to find Elizabeth, practically buried by leaves and pine needles. Brandy must have gotten there before he had time to complete the scheme or they may not have found her at all.

Joseph was near hysteria by then. "Take it easy, big fellow," Emily soothed. "We aren't going to hurt her."

They checked her out gently and discovered that she had a wound in one of her wings near her body. She was still able to flap her wing which was a good sign, but she would need some help and much care.

They rolled out the canvas stretcher from the bag, bound Elizabeth with ropes and placed her on it for transfer back to the jeep. Her eyes were filled with fear and her heart was racing. They talked to her as gently as possible so as to calm and reassure her.

Joseph followed, his plaintive cries of despair torturing them. When they drove the jeep (more slowly this time) back toward the refuge, he followed, honking anxiously.

They sedated Elizabeth and repaired her wing. Fortunately, the Martins had been drunk and most of the buckshot had missed her. They felt that she would be fine but it would take two or three weeks of recuperation to know for sure. By then, the weather would be too severe for the geese to continue their southern migration. There would be no problem with the recovery except for the male. If they could just capture him also, and keep him with her until she could be released in the spring...

TALES FROM THE SUNROOM

Later that night, Joseph crept silently around the barn where Elizabeth lay captive. He had no idea if she was okay, but he knew she was in there.

"Elizabeth?" he cried softly, "are you okay? Elizabeth?"

She was still groggy from the sedation, but she heard him calling to her. "I'm here, Joseph, and I'm okay. I'm locked up but they didn't hurt me. My wing is all bound up though and I can't fly!"

"I'm going to try to get you out of there, Elizabeth, but just try to stay calm. I won't leave you, no matter what. I'll stay right here until I can get you out."

"Oh, Joseph," she sobbed, "I'm so frightened."

"I know, my love, I know," he soothed. "So am I but we'll try to get out of this mess as soon as we can. Try not to worry, and just rest as much as you can. You'll need your strength when we get you out of there."

Joseph stayed close to the barn each day but would not allow either of the women to approach him. They placed food out for him and he eventually ate it out of sheer necessity. He was starving. The women spoke kindly to him but he did not trust them. They were Elizabeth's captors so he kept his distance.

It took ten days of cajoling, feeding and scheming but they finally captured Joseph after placing a mild sedative in his food one morning. He was so exhausted from the emotional stress that he became lethargic soon after consuming the medication. He was still no pushover to capture but they managed to get him into a large cage which they set beside Elizabeth in the warm barn.

His dismay at also being captured was somewhat soothed when he saw his beloved mate. They honked and hissed gently to each other. They strained to touch each other, so the two women carefully slid Joseph's cage closer to his mate's. They had no cage large enough to house both of them so this was the

Come the Spring

best accommodation they could manage. They reached out and were close enough that their beaks could touch. Joseph even managed to get his wing into her cage so as to stroke her lovingly. Both women were deeply touched when they saw this, and they kept them as close beside each other as possible.

Joseph was distraught with their situation but felt helpless to change it. He sensed kindness from these humans but couldn't understand why they were being held in bondage. He and Elizabeth were fed and watered daily and their cages were cleaned. Elizabeth's wounds had healed, and as the cold weeks passed, he knew it would soon be time to return to their lake in New York.

It was a brutal winter in the mountains that year. It became a challenge on some days to forge through the high snowdrifts and furious winds from the house to the barn in order to feed the animals. The women began leaving extra food and water on the days they could break through. Creatures, except for pampered pets, will not overeat so it was possible to leave extra rations without being concerned that all the food would be consumed at once.

"Joseph," Elizabeth asked softly, "do you think we'll ever get out of here and go home?"

"I don't know," he whispered in reply. "I don't know. At least we're together." He tried to remain upbeat but his heart just wasn't in it.

Finally, Emily and Brandy decided it was time to release the geese and hope that the female would be strong enough to leave. They knew that geese bred in March or April and it was already a few days into the month of March.

They were fed twice on the last day of their captivity in hopes they would eat the extra rations, and both Elizabeth and Joseph sensed that something was about to happen. The air about them seemed to crackle with excitement.

The women decided to release the female first to make certain she could fly. They opened her cage, she dashed out and spread her wings. She turned, realized that Joseph was still imprisoned, and stopped. She paced around nervously.

"Well," observed Emily, "looks like we're going to have to let him out before she'll try her wings."

"Looks like," agreed Brandy.

They opened his cage, and he erupted from his cell. He rushed to Elizabeth and they danced ecstatically around each other, dipping their heads, entwining their necks, rubbing their beaks together. The women laughed uncontrollably at the theatrics.

The two raced down the drive together, lifted into the air, and were soon flying away toward home. Together.

It took four days for Joseph and Elizabeth to reach their New York home from West Virginia. They moved slowly, stopping frequently for Elizabeth to rest, reveling in the joy of being free and together.

They built their nest on the opposite shore of the bay just as Elizabeth had planned the year before. It seemed like eons ago, so much had happened. Joseph stayed close to her, often casting his eyes in her direction to make certain she was still there and well.

"Joseph," came the familiar tone, "come the spring..."

Joseph smiled to himself, honked tenderly, and waited for her instructions.

The Gray Lady

The Lord is near to the brokenhearted, and saves the crushed in spirit.

                              Psalms 34:18

Denise Fuller stood outside the front door of their newly acquired home and relished the excitement of moving day. She marveled at the intricate woodworking on the baseboards and crown moldings. The wide pine boards on the foyer floor were warmly stained by time and the footsteps of countless residents and visitors.

As she opened the ancient door and stepped inside, she was struck by incredibly cold air. How strange, she wondered. The hot July day was heavy and muggy so she attributed it to a glitch in the central air conditioning and dismissed it in the confusion and commotion of moving furniture in.

She and Charlie had bought the house, sight unseen, from the internet when they learned they were to be transferred to historic Salisbury by Charlie's employer. The pictures of the spacious kitchen, huge fireplaces and high ceilings captivated them immediately. They realized the potential problems with an older home, and this one was over 150 years old, but the house's biography indicated new wiring, plumbing and a new heating/air

TALES FROM THE SUNROOM

conditioning system. In addition, full house insulation had been installed, all within the past 5 years, and a new roof had been added 7 years ago, so it seemed too good to be true. They jumped at the opportunity and their excitement mounted as moving day approached.

Shortly after moving in, the family began to experience strange incidents. Spencer, 5, and Madison, 3, began to whine and fret, which was quite unusual for them. They had both been very happy and well adjusted up to this point, but neither was sleeping well.

Charlie kept losing his car keys, and his shoes were missing from his closet each morning. Sometimes he would find them in the bathroom, the den downstairs under the sofa, or even tossed into the fireplace. And the car keys were extremely difficult to locate. He even found them inside one of his lost shoes one morning.

Denise's uneasiness increased, especially regarding the children. They kept talking about the gray lady who came to see them at night. At first, she dismissed it as childish make believe but they kept mentioning this gray lady.

"What does she say to you?" Denise gently inquired, not wishing to alarm the children.

"She says to stay here and not go out with Daddy," Spencer answered. There was fear in his eyes as he caught the expression on Denise's face. Her children were her life and she abhorred anything that harmed or threatened them in any fashion. Her eyes filled with tears, and they sensed her anxiety, throwing themselves tearfully into her arms.

"I scared, Mommy," implored little Madison.

Denise began taking the children into their bedroom at night to sleep with her and Charlie. She wasn't comfortable with that solution but felt it was necessary for the well being of the chil-

The Gray Lady

dren. Something frightening was in the house, and she could not rest until they identified it.

Charlie awakened each morning to shower in preparation for work. Frequently, as he showered, the cold water would mysteriously cease running, and he would be burned by hot water. Denise would hear him scream, and she began dreading his being in the shower. He even turned the temperature down on the hot water heater in the basement, but it would be turned back up with no feasible explanation as to how it happened. He finally had to start bathing in the bathtub which increased his irritability. Denise had no problem with the water in the shower, but she was afraid to risk placing the children in there and also bathed them in the tub.

As Charlie stepped out of the tub one morning, he was shocked to find his bathrobe missing. He distinctly remembered wearing it into the room and removing it as he stepped into his bath. He had tossed it over a chair behind the tub. He looked around and found it stuffed behind the commode on the other side of the room. He ran his fingers through his hair in exasperation as he retrieved it, and moved back into the bedroom to dress. Denise and the children had already gone to the kitchen, and he could hear them chatting downstairs, so he knew they had nothing to do with moving his robe. Why would they want to anyway? None of this made sense.

He finished dressing, put on his tie, and reached for his shoes which he had placed under the bed the night before. Once again, his shoes were missing. He went to the top of the stairs and shouted down to Denise, "Denise, are my shoes down there anywhere?"

"Hold on for a minute and I'll look!"

Shortly, she came to the bottom of the stairs, looked up at him helplessly, and stated, "No, they aren't, Charlie."

He stood there and they gazed at each other silently for several seconds before he turned and went back into the bedroom. There at the side of the bed were his shoes. He tossed his arms into the air and cried in despair, "What is going on in this damned house?"

He pulled his shoes on quickly and fled downstairs. As he passed by the mirror on the large, antique wardrobe against the wall in their bedroom, he caught a glimpse of a shadow from across the room. He whirled around but saw nothing there.

"No time for breakfast, honey. Just pour some coffee in my thermos cup. I'll grab something before I get to the office. Have you seen my keys?"

Their eyes met across the room and Charlie was close to exploding by then. They moved around the downstairs, searching for the elusive keys, finally locating them behind the curtains in the living room.

"That does it," Charlie retorted. "From now on, I'm hiding the keys outside so I don't have to go through this everyday!"

The incidents became more frequent after the children began sleeping in their parents' bedroom. It reached the final breaking point one day when Charlie started to leave the house to take the children to the park on an outing. He was unable to open the front door. It was stuck fast and only after great effort and tugging and pulling, was he able to force it open. The children began screaming and sobbing fearfully, and Spencer shouted, "I'm cold, Daddy!"

Denise came running to protect and comfort the children just as Charlie forced the door open. He scooped up Spencer, Denise grasped Madison to her breast, and they ran from the house. As they left, a vase crashed by Charlie, narrowly missing his head.

"What's going on?" queried Charlie, obviously shaken. Denise

The Gray Lady

was nearly hysterical and only her concern for the children kept her from screaming.

"I don't know, Charlie, but we can't take the children back in there. Not now. Not until we know what's going on."

"I agree," he nodded. "We'll go to a motel and I'll get some inspector in here to find out what's wrong."

"Inspectors won't find the problem, Charlie, because it isn't mechanical. I'm going to talk to Rev. Jones."

"Denise, there's no such thing as ghosts and you'll just look ridiculous," he scolded.

Denise was a little surprised at his response as no mention of ghosts had ever been made. "I don't care how ridiculous I look, Charlie. My children are frightened, and I'm telling you there's something sinister in that house, and I won't take them back until we get rid of it!"

He knew she meant it but he still grumbled. She went back into the house, quickly gathered what they would need for a few days, and left without a backward glance.

They spent the afternoon at the park, allowing the children to relax and calm down. They sat in a gazebo, talking quietly about the strange incidents which had occurred, as the children played.

The unexplainable coldness in the foyer, Charlie's missing keys and shoes which could just as easily reappear, the hot water in Charlie's shower, the hot water heater temperature being inexplicably turned up after being turned down. Also, the strange visits from the gray lady warning the children not to leave with their father along with the front door refusing to open when they tried to leave earlier, and the vase flying across the room, barely missing Charlie's head. There were also the strange shadows which Charlie would see in the mirrors from time to time. He was beginning to doubt his sanity.

TALES FROM THE SUNROOM

Denise sat there beside Charlie, watching the children and gazing at the lake beyond them. A dragonfly skimmed gracefully across the water's surface, landing briefly. She marveled at how he could accomplish this feat without sinking. The sun glinted on his nearly transparent wings, giving him a look of majesty. She needed this scene to bring her back into reality, the reality that the world was an orderly place with a purpose and meaning for everything. They just had to find out what the purpose and meaning of the force in their home was.

Her attention was drawn back to the present as Charlie continued speaking.

He reluctantly admitted that he had experienced strange attacks from soon after they moved in. His keys and shoes were nuisances but once when he was using a knife in the kitchen, the knife seemed to take on a life of its own, and he had to struggle to keep it from slashing his arm. He walked by a mirror in the upstairs hallway once and caught a glimpse of a strange and menacing apparition. It seemed to be threatening him in some way and made him quite uneasy.

After spending the night in a motel, Denise and the children went to the Episcopal Church they attended, requesting to see Father Jones. Charlie had gone to work, so she left the children at the church daycare center and went in to see the minister. He welcomed her warmly and asked about the family. She immediately began weeping and he moved quickly to her side in comfort and concern.

"I'm sorry, Father," she apologized. "It's just that I'm so frightened."

She explained what had been happening, and he was obviously shaken and concerned by her revelations. He made no attempt to discount her story and accepted her descriptions as genuine. She felt completely at ease and was flooded with relief

The Gray Lady

by his acceptance. She needed to know that her fears were not hysterical delusions.

After listening to her, he asked, "Have you done any research on the house?"

"No, just the biography which was on the internet and it made no mention of being haunted or any past problems."

"What is the address?"

"It's 109 Fisherman Lane," she replied.

"Let's go to the library and do some research," he suggested. "Salisbury has a long, distinguished history and the Historic Society and the library take great pride in recording historic facts and legends."

Of course, thought Denise as she smiled in agreement. What a wise and wonderful idea. Better than calling in inspectors! Or ghost busters!

She felt great relief that the vicar had taken charge and offered plans of action. She was ready to let someone else take control as she and Charlie were at their wits end.

She gathered up the children and couldn't help but notice how happy and relaxed they were. There was no fear in their eyes and faces. Guilt tugged at her heart as she held them close.

Spencer and Madison looked at books and watched cartoons on TV as Denise and Father Jones sought the history of 109 Fisherman Lane. One family caught their attention because of the tragedy which befell them, as well as the parallel of their names with the Fuller family.

Their names were Charlie and Sarah Madison, and they were living in the house during the Civil War, under the constant fear of attack. Denise felt a chill when she saw their names. They had two children – reportedly a boy and a girl – but their names were not recorded there. It was late 1864 (the exact date was not recorded) and Charlie Madison had taken the children out of the house for some reason. They were riding in a carriage when they were attacked by a group of marauders. They were all shot and Charlie's coin purse and watch were stolen. The children died instantly and Charlie died at home three days later.

They asked the librarian about the family, and she suggested they call Mrs. Boynton. Sadie Boynton was the city's historic expert and often assisted the library in its research.

Father Jones called Mrs. Boynton, briefly explained the situation and scheduled an appointment for the next afternoon. Denise felt much better as she and the children left the library and Father Jones to return to the motel.

The next afternoon, she left the children at St. Martins' as she picked up the vicar, and they met with Mrs. Boynton in her home.

She was a personable, elderly lady with a twinkle in her eye and a lilt in her step, despite her advanced years. Her demeanor and appearance belied her almost 90 years. She delighted in talking to interested people about her beloved city, and welcomed them warmly. Her home was lovely and well cared for, and was filled with Victorian furnishings. She served them tea from a bone china set so transparent, it reminded Denise of the wings of the dragonfly she had seen the day before at the city lake. She had never lived in a small town before, and she was surprised and intrigued each day as she realized the relationships within her community. It was as if everything and everyone was connected in spirit.

Perhaps, thought Denise, it's that way everywhere but in a small town, I have more time to recognize it. And people have more time to know each other.

She was becoming more and more comfortable in her new hometown and hoped they would be able to stay in their lovely old Victorian home.

The Gray Lady

Mrs. Boynton listened intently as they gave her the story of the family's experiences since moving into the home barely two months earlier. As they finished, she slowly set her teacup down, rose from her chair, and moved to a large bookcase on the far side of the room. She searched the large collection for several minutes, and then retrieved a thick, dusty volume.

"If memory serves me, that was the Madison family," she declared.

Denise and Father Jones looked at each other with surprise and relief. They had not mentioned the information they had uncovered at the library. Maybe she could help them. She returned with the book, and commented, "So you felt cold air in the foyer?"

"Yes!" Denise answered excitedly, moving to the edge of her chair in her excitement. "But nowhere else."

"This is a book published by my great-grandfather, Davis Boynton, back in 1904. His grandmother knew most of the people in this area, and she kept meticulous records."

She leafed through the pages, concentrated on one area, and then announced, "Here it is!"

They gathered around to read the account. The Madisons married and moved to 109 Fisherman Lane in 1857. He was a banker and they were very prominent in Salisbury. Sarah and Charlie hosted frequent social events, and by 1859, they had two children – a boy named Spencer and a daughter named Marie.

Denise gasped audibly as she heard the names of the children. Madison's middle name was Marie. And Spencer!

After the Civil War began, the bank closed and the family fell on hard times. Charlie did not go to fight because he was stricken with arthritis. He used a cane to walk and would sometimes have to use a wheelchair when it was cold weather.

On a particularly warm day in November, 1864, Charlie took

the children for a ride in the carriage. Sarah was taking care of her sick mother and didn't want Charlie to take the children, but they begged so passionately. They had been locked behind the doors of their home for weeks and really needed to escape.

It was on this outing that they were attacked by marauders. Neighbors brought them back home and helped Sarah bury her beloved children. Three days later she buried Charlie and shortly thereafter, her mother.

Sarah was never the same, and would often be seen standing on the widow's walk outside the attic window, waiting for Charlie and the children. She became reclusive and bitter, and locals began calling her the gray lady because of her ashen skin and dark clothing.

After her death, there were reports of seeing her on the widow's walk on some nights. There were also reports of coldness in the foyer which greeted any new arrival. Some residents of the home reported seeing an apparition from time to time but there were never any attacks. Not until now.

Mrs. Boynton observed that with all the coincidences of the names of the Fuller family, Sarah may have thought her family had finally returned. Charlie Madison and Charlie Fuller. Spencer Madison and Spencer Fuller. And not only did little Madison have their last name but her middle name was the same as Sarah's beloved daughter, Marie Madison.

Perhaps Sarah was attempting to protect her children from her Charlie's reckless decision to go for a ride so she hid Charlie Fuller's keys and shoes to keep him home, and she had warned the children not to leave with him. She attempted to keep him in when he tried to leave with the children on their last day in the house. She was punishing him for her pain on the other times with the hot water and the knife.

Denise was relieved but understandably concerned. "What

The Gray Lady

do we do now, Father?"

"We'll talk to Sarah and tell her it's okay to go on to her family. She can do no more for them here, and her place is with them on the other side."

Denise and Father Jones thanked Mrs. Boynton for her information and her insight as they left. They planned to go back to 109 Fisherman Lane that afternoon.

As they entered later that day, they noticed a sense of expectancy and anxiety within the house. The Father suggested that Denise talk to Sarah, since she, too, was a mother of two children and may hear Denise's words more readily than the vicar's.

"Sarah, we understand your fear and concern about our being here. I know you're confused, and I appreciate that you are trying to protect my children, but I assure you they are in no danger. You're confused about your children and my children. Spencer and Madison are my children, and I know you've been looking for your Spencer and Marie for many years.

"The truth is, Sarah, they've been gone for over 100 years, and I'm certain they're waiting for you on the other side. There's nothing else you can do for them here, and I know you don't mean to, but you're frightening my children, and my husband.

"Charlie Fuller is my husband. Your Charlie has gone to the other side with your children, Sarah. What happened was not his fault. It was an act of war and violence, and I doubt that anyone could have stopped it. I'm sorry it happened, Sarah, I truly am, but you've done everything that you can here. It's time for you to join them on the other side. We love your home and will always care for it, but we need to know that we can have peace here. And the only way we can have that peace, is for you to leave our home."

Denise paused and they listened intently for some sign or sound or sight that Sarah could hear and understand them.

TALES FROM THE SUNROOM

Father Jones added, "God has promised you and your Charlie and your children that we will all have eternal life with Him, Sarah. Charlie and Spencer and Marie are with Him now, and they want you to be there also."

They stood in silence for what seemed an eternity, and then they seemed to hear a deep, soulful sigh. A breeze moved by them, gently bumping the screen door as it passed through, and rustled the leaves in the elm trees standing near the steps. They looked at each other and smiled in relief.

"I believe she's gone," Father Jones declared.

Several days later, the Fuller family returned to 109 Fisherman Lane. When they opened the front door and entered, they immediately noticed there was no coldness. The children were somewhat apprehensive, but were soon running through the house, searching out their toys and other treasures left behind so hastily a few days earlier. Denise and Charlie could sense a difference, a peacefulness in the house. They embraced, knowing that they were at home at last.

Sometime later, Denise found a portrait of a Victorian family which represented a family as a father, mother and two young children. The father had a cane, the mother was beautiful and the children were dressed so as to make their gender indiscernible, but it struck Denise that the Madison family must have looked much like this.

She purchased the portrait and hung it in the foyer for all to see as they entered. It seemed a fitting memorial to the Madison family, and a gentle reminder that they had once lived, loved, laughed and died in this house.

The Guide

Open my mind so that I may perceive truth with an unseeing eye.

—g. gurley

Abbe grabbed the ringing phone impatiently, answering with the bite of frustration in her voice.

"You're wanted in the courtroom," the voice on the other end of the line demanded.

"Okay, okay, I'll be right there."

She was a state probation officer and was experienced enough to know that such a call didn't necessarily mean that a probation violation hearing before the judge was imminent. Chances were, she'd spend several hours sitting there while favored attorneys pushed their cases ahead of hers. But she did know that regardless of that fact, she was required to be present when summoned.

She scooped up a number of files, a note pad and pen, rushed out, explaining to the secretary over her shoulder as she left, "I'll be in court." No further explanation was needed or expected.

Two hours later she returned to her office. It took 37 seconds for her testimony in this case and less than one minute for the two year sentence to be invoked against the probationer, who was in violation of the court ordered conditions.

TALES FROM THE SUNROOM

It seemed so pointless, and even heartless, to Abbe. This was a human being who was unable to conform to the norms of society for whatever reason, and consequently, had had to face the inevitable fate of arrest, conviction, probation, and now prison. She usually felt somewhat guilty and responsible when this happened even though common sense and logic told her that she was not, and could not, be responsible for the actions of others.

However, she frequently asked herself if maybe she missed something which may have been helpful. More treatment for drug and alcohol abuse. A different counseling technique to reach that person. Would a referral to a psychiatrist have identified the damage to his or her psyche? More schooling, training, a different job, a different living arrangement.

Steve Burch, a very wise and insightful peer, once cautioned her, "You didn't break it, Abbe, and you can't always fix it."

That simple advice gave her great comfort, and she frequently recalled it when she lost a case, but the small nagging doubt was ever present that, just perhaps, she may have done more.

She rested her head in her hands for a moment, ignoring briefly the pile of telephone messages which had accumulated during her absence. Her respite was broken by the ringing of the telephone.

"This is Officer Young," she quipped.

"Officer Young, this is Bill Black, an attorney here in town. I'd like to talk to you about a client of mine who's been charged with breaking and entering. He's a good candidate for probation and the district attorney suggested I speak to you before we go to court next week..."

The stress of her job continued to prey on Abbe. She was unable to sleep well, and she would awaken around 4AM each morning, going over in her mind what duties had to be completed on that day. She was irritable with her family, withdrawn

The Guide

from her co-workers. Even worse, she began to lose her ability to focus her attention on clients when they talked to her.

She sought the aid of a local counselor who specialized in stress management. A psychological evaluation indicated that Abbe was borderline depressed, so Jan, her counselor, paid special attention to her immediate needs. Usually, group sessions were conducted for stress management but several private sessions were desirable for Abbe.

Abbe eagerly attended these sessions and blossomed under the new-found techniques. She learned how to recognize and release tension in her whole body. It was particularly evident in her clenched, cold fists. Her hands became warm for the first time in many months, and she became kinder to her family, as well as regaining the ability to approach her peers.

She knew that they too harbored these same tensions, anxieties and fears. She began to gather strength and regained her positive attitude and happy demeanor.

She moved on to the group training sessions and attained even more exciting and enlightening knowledge. It was in a deep relaxation exercise that she had her first experience with visualization.

She found herself standing in the center of a massive wheat field. The wheat was thick and filled with abundant fruit. It moved gently in an invisible breeze, and this movement was tranquil, peaceful and comforting to Abbe. The gold of the stems, pregnant with kernels, shimmered and glistened as they silently rippled to and fro in the white light. There was no intense heat, nor blinding glare, as from the sun she knew; but just a comfortable, friendly presence encompassing the scene. Tiny butterflies fluttered about and several lighted on Abbe's shoulders as well as her outstretched hand.

Ahead and to the left, she spied a large, expansive oak, and

TALES FROM THE SUNROOM

her first thought was, This must be the tree of life.

She moved toward it, noting there was no exertion to her legs as she walked. The wheat shafts offered no resistance, receding noiselessly and closing silently behind her with no trace of her entry and passage visible.

She was struck not only by the tranquility and unobtrusive light, but also by the melodic silence. She had never experienced silence which offered a song, but this silence seemed to be filled with an inaudible music. It wasn't anything she heard with her ears and could describe with her memory, but was more of a message to her spirit. She heard it with her heart, her soul, her faith, and not the physical appendages which had detected sound for her before this place.

She arrived at the tree in what seemed to be an instant but could just as easily have been an hour. There was no concept of time as she knew it. The butterflies remained with her, and she smiled as her gaze traveled to the thick canopy of lush vegetation cloaking the massive limbs of this ancient monument. Even though the leaves were dense and compact, she noticed no dark shade beneath them. There was just the same soothing, loving white light.

The trunk of the tree encompassed a large portion of space without any indication of intrusion or overpowering presence, but just the feeling of a great majesty which was in its rightful place within the universe. Huge roots wound around the perimeter and formed a niche, which seemed to invite Abbe to enter.

She entered the nook and sank comfortably against the brownness of the tree. There was no roughness or distress from the thick bark, just softness akin to a comfortable and loving embrace.

She was reluctant to leave this peaceful sanctuary, but soon found her own complex domain easier to connect with after being revived in her wheat field. She knew that she would be able to seek solace there when necessary, but the rejuvenation she experienced strengthened her for many months.

After the visit to the wheat field, Abbe was more contemplative. She was still impatient, but learned tolerance and a deeper respect, became more cognizant of the silent communication behind the words spoken by others, especially when talking to her clients.

She had only superficial knowledge of their lifestyles and childhood histories. She believed in the resiliency and stamina of the human spirit, and she could not even imagine the horrors some of these individuals must have endured which led to their social failures.

Being chastised and even locked away by the very society which nurtured and protected her was hateful to Abbe, and the pressures that pushed someone to that point must have been horrendous and completely beyond her comprehension, if not her understanding. There had to be an explanation, however elusive, of why there was a personal breakdown and nonconformity on such a large scale, which devoured so many individuals. It led one to believe that perhaps society's mores had become unobtainable for much of the population.

She learned to accept the person and reject the behavior. However, in doing so, she was forced to compromise her own principles, thus increasing her personal stress level. She felt her apprehension level expanding, so she once again retreated to her deep relaxation exercises at her next group session. Jan cautioned each member not to attempt this method alone until they became extremely familiar and comfortable with the results, as it could be frightening or threatening to the inexperienced novice.

Abbe approached her wheat field with lighthearted relief and gleeful expectancy. But this time it was different. Instead of a wheat field, there was the large oak tree with a small stream bubbling by it. She was surprised, but not unpleasantly so, and curious. She moved eagerly, yet slowly so as to savor each bit and piece of the scenery.

She noticed that she was barefooted, and was walking across small, rounded pebbles on the bank of the stream; however, there was no pain or discomfort. Actually, there was no feeling at all – just a sensation of movement; almost like floating. She smiled broadly at this revelation.

She stepped lightly and confidently into the stream, and was able to view her feet through the clear, sparkling surface. But once again, there was no discomfort or even moisture from what she perceived to be cool water. It was really quite pleasant. She stood there, embracing the joy of this new feeling.

She gradually became aware of another presence to her left . As her mind grasped this knowledge, she processed that the tree was on her right side, so she could only assume that this presence came from the opposite side of the stream from Abbe's point of entry.

She was a female figure, standing several inches taller than Abbe, dressed in a long, white robe. She was likewise barefooted and standing in the water. The bottom of her robe was submerged in the stream and moved gently as the waters flowed by. Abbe immediately noticed that, like her own feet, this entity's feet, as well as robe, appeared to be unaffected by the wetness of the water.

There was a soothing, kind aura surrounding the being, and even though her features were misty through the soft glow about her, Abbe had the distinct impression that she was beautiful beyond earthly standards. She felt immediately at ease and comfortable in her presence. It was almost like seeing an old and

The Guide

trusted friend, or coming home after a long and rocky absence.

"Who are you?" Abbe inquired softly, reaching out her hand in an irresistible urge to make tangible contact.

"I am your Guide," she answered with a loving smile. She allowed Abbe's hand to rest on her arm. The arm was covered with the long sleeve of the robe, but Abbe could feel her soft, warm flesh without the obstruction of the fabric. It existed, yet it didn't. Strangely, Abbe wasn't disturbed or even confused by this knowledge. It just seemed correct and proper and not anything which needed to be questioned. It was three-dimensional faith.

"Do I know you?" Curiously, she felt as if she did.

"I have always been and will always be with you, Abbe."

It was such a simple concept which rang so true that Abbe had no need to question further. They moved easily down the stream, walking side by side.

"Where did you come from?"

She made no reply but gazed kindly into Abbe's eyes and placed the tips of her fingers gently over Abbe's heart.

Abbe understood.

They walked another distance. She stopped, looked beyond her Guide, and inquired, "What's over there?" pointing to the opposite side of the stream.

"That's not for you now, Abbe. Later, when the time is right." Her voice, though not stern, sounded final and gently firm. Abbe questioned no more.

As they moved on, the Guide asked her, "What do you need, Abbe, above everything else, to make you happy?"

Without hesitation, she answered, "Patience."

The Guide smiled wisely, pleased with her request. She leaned over, picked up one of the smooth, round, white stones from the stream and pressed it into Abbe's right hand.

TALES FROM THE SUNROOM

"Just as this water has over time worn this stone smooth and round, so will time bring you the patience you seek."

She looked down at the small orb in her hand and rolled it over gently. She could feel its smooth hardness against her flesh just as she had been able to feel her Guide's arm. She was surprised by the tangible substance of the arm and the stone since nothing else in this dimension had been so.

She looked up to question this phenomenon, but discovered that the Guide was gone. She had neither seen nor heard her departure. She peered to the far side of the stream, attempting to see beyond the shore, since she was convinced she had disappeared there. The only presence was a milky white concealment which her eyes could not penetrate. It was nothing physical which she could name, but was a type of shade between her and what was beyond this cover. She didn't feel locked out, but acknowledged that it was a private place which she could enter at another time.

She moved to the now comfortable security of the huge oak. She sank easily and effortlessly into the familiar restfulness of the niche to reflect on what had occurred. She continued to be delighted and enchanted by the almost floating sensation of her movements. They offered no exertion or struggle, and she experienced no tiredness or discomfort from these motions. Her settling into the roots of the tree reinforced this belief. She felt as if she could walk forever without being tired.

Abbe felt comforted and soothed by her encounter with her Guide. She began to realize just how ridiculous and non-productive her worries, concerns and fears about others really were. She was attempting to change things and circumstances and people she was ill-equipped to change, situations beyond her comprehension or complete understanding, which were all being monitored by another dimension. Her comfort and relief were

The Guide

the direct result of these revelations, and she sensed a magnificent sense of relief that she was able to abandon her useless worrying, without relinquishing her human concern, for her fellowman. It was her duty and responsibility to accept on faith that which she could not alter. She understood that she was being somewhat arrogant in thinking that she could control and change others' actions and behaviors.

Abbe had been promised by her Guide that which she longed for – patience. She suddenly realized that most of her impatience was with herself, and what she perceived to be her personal inadequacies. It was heartwarming, and the experience with her Guide was sustenance for her soul.

She had been promised patience. And she knew that it would be so. She smiled as she thought of something she had once read. A woman had prayed for patience. "Lord, give me patience. And hurry!"

Not on my own timetable, she thought, but when the time is right. It felt good to relinquish the burden of responsibility for that which she could not control.

The Transient

Helping the helpless is not charity – it's humanity.

—g. gurley

Jenny Roberts answered the bell at the window in the police department's records division late one cold winter afternoon to find a disheveled, meek looking gentleman standing there, obviously cold and probably hungry. There was a sadness and humbleness projected from his eyes that caught her offguard. She was accustomed to seeing angry or frightened or confused or desperate, and yes, even sad, but seldom did she see humble, sad and meek. The sight touched her.

"May I help you?" she asked kindly, pushing the auditory button from behind the bulletproof glass so that he could hear her.

"Um, yes ma'am, I'm passing through town and was wondering if there's a place where I can get a quick meal."

She understood immediately, smiled warmly at him, and replied, "Yes, sir, there's a place about 6 blocks from here. You can get a meal there and stay the night if you need to. They serve meals at 7AM, noon and 6PM."

She stopped short of identifying the facility as the local night shelter for the homeless. There was something dignified about

TALES FROM THE SUNROOM

his demeanor, a presence which evoked respect.

He looked up at the clock on the wall, noting that it was 2:30PM. She could tell that his need was urgent, and 6:00 must have seemed a long way off. She knew that what she was thinking was against departmental policy, but she went out on a limb. All of the personnel were kind, caring professionals who genuinely cared about the people they served, so she took a chance.

"If you'd like, you can have a seat for awhile until they open instead of going out in the cold. Would you like a cup of coffee?"

His face lit up with gratitude. "Yes ma'am, a cup of coffee would be very welcomed, and I'd be in your debt." He sat down in one of the chairs lining the wall, and she could tell from the way he sank into it that he was virtually exhausted.

"Lieutenant, I'll be right back," she explained.

He had heard her conversation and her invitation but made no comment. They all understood Jenny's compassion, but they also knew she was no pushover. They respected her ability to reach out to the helpless while still being able to control the ruthless. These attributes made her a valuable member of the department which she had served for more than 20 years. She was experienced in recognizing human emotions and pains, and this experience endeared her to her co-workers, eliminating the need to scrutinize or question her judgment.

Jenny moved down the hall to the coffee pot. There were always snacks and goodies surrounding this oasis, and fortunately, today was no exception. She found a leftover country ham biscuit which she popped into the microwave, a banana and three chocolate cookies. She quickly placed them on a paper plate, topped it with a napkin, poured the coffee and placed a packet of sugar along with a small container of cream on top, and hurried to the lobby. Captain Miller saw her approach the door leading

The Transient

to the lobby, had an immediate idea of what was happening, and pushed the door open for her. She smiled her thanks at him as their eyes met in the unspoken communication individuals working with the troubled and downtrodden develop over time.

She handed the food to the gentleman who looked on the brink of collapse. As she approached, he scrambled to his feet, nodding his head in respect and total gratefulness.

"We had a few things left in our breakroom," she explained. "I hope you don't mind my bringing them out. I don't like to see waste. I wasn't sure how you like your coffee so I brought sugar and cream for you. If you need more, please let me know. We have plenty." She babbled so as to avoid his being embarrassed by her gesture.

"Oh, thank you ma'am! I really appreciate this." He thanked her enthusiastically.

She was touched by his enthusiasm and his sincerity. Her eyes were misted as she smiled and turned to the door, swiping her electronic pass over it so that it would open to her. She regained control as she returned to work, assumed her place at the window and noticed that he had already consumed the food.

She was offduty at 3:30, and as the time approached, she made a decision. She would take him to the shelter so he wouldn't have to stand in the cold so long. It didn't open until 5:00 so she would have to stay there for awhile but she had nothing pressing to do at home. She called and left a message on the answering machine for Roger.

"Honey, I'm going to be a little late tonight. I have something to do after work and should be there no later than 5:30. See ya! Love ya!"

Lt. Billings heard her, got up from his desk and approached her desk. "Jenny, you aren't planning to take that man to the shelter, are you?"

"Yes, sir, I am," she admitted. Darn! she thought to herself. You can't have a private conversation anywhere around a bunch of cops!

"No, I'm sorry, Jenny, but I can't allow that. We know nothing at all about him." He saw the look on her face, braced himself for the argument he saw coming, and raised his hand to block her response.

"I'll take him myself when I get off at 4:30," he promised.

Relief flooded her face. "Thank you, Lt."

At 3:30, she returned to the lobby and sat beside him. He was somewhat uneasy when she sat down, but she soon put him at ease.

"My name is Jenny Roberts. I live here in Henson with my husband and our dog. Our daughter and grandchildren live in Detroit. What's your name?"

Her forthrightness surprised him but also invited him to relax.

"Stuart. Stuart Samuels."

She sat there visiting with him until the Lieutenant came to transport him to the shelter. Her genuineness and open honesty enveloped him with warmth and comfort, and it was a very pleasant visit for them both. She was, however, unable to learn little more than his name. He was unwilling to share any personal information beyond who he was. There was no suspicion in his behavior, but rather a well-guarded, imperceptible wall had been erected around his persona, a wall he guarded with a nearly involuntary custom, which had evolved over a long, painful period of time. The habit of time decreed that this wall would be impenetrable, and it would take a uniquely resolute individual or situation to defeat that invisible barrier.

She spent a restless night worrying about Mr. Samuels. She

The Transient

was quite perturbed with herself, as she knew better than to worry about the people with whom she dealt. The majority of them were incapable of adjusting to the mores of society, so they consequently existed precariously outside the norms of that society with little support, encouragement or hope.

However, there was something unique and wonderful about Mr. Samuels. He was not the usual vagrant stumbling through life, hooked on drugs or alcohol. There was a gentleness, an intense intelligence and eloquence which were evident in their brief conversation. There was a genuine person behind the sadness and tragedy.

She picked up the phone and called the shelter. The director answered, and she was relieved that he had. She knew him quite well and felt more comfortable in talking with him than one of the many volunteers. Terry would more readily share information with her.

"Terry, this is Jenny Roberts. How are you?"

"I'm well, Jenny, how are you?" Terry Donavan was obviously glad to hear her voice. She was a good friend to the shelter.

"Terry, Lt. Billings brought a gentleman down there last night around 4:30 and I'm wondering if he's still there. His name is Stuart Samuels."

"Let me check the roster, Jenny. Why, what's he wanted for?"

"No, no," she quickly assured him. "He just impressed me yesterday, and I was a little worried about him."

"Um, let me see—Samuels, Samuels," he spoke thoughtfully as he searched the list. "Yes, here he is. He hasn't checked out yet, and as a matter of fact, he left with the van from the temporary agency this morning to go to work. There's no indication here that he won't be back."

The local temporary agency sent their company van to the shelter each morning to pick up men who wanted to work. There

TALES FROM THE SUNROOM

was work for all of them for a few days at a time. Nothing was permanent but usually the residents of the night shelter weren't looking for permanent work.

"Great!" She was obviously relieved. "I'll be down there at supper time to help serve. Maybe I can see him then."

"Okay, Jenny, we'll be glad to have your help," he replied gratefully.

Jenny went to the computer on her break and keyed in as much information as she could on Mr. Samuels. All she had was his name, race and sex, but she hoped to find something, anything on him. If he was wanted or had ever been convicted of a felony in the U. S., chances were she would get a hit on his name. She found nothing and she wasn't sure if she was glad or disappointed. There was chaos of emotions, ranging from relief to dashed hopes.

Lt. Billings stopped behind her and noticed what she was doing. "Try the missing persons website," he suggested.

"Great idea! I don't understand why people don't like you, Lt!" she teased.

She immediately keyed in the data and waited impatiently. She watched the tiny blue bar on the bottom of the screen as it slowly (agonizingly so) filled up. It was 19%, 38%, 62%, 89%, and suddenly, the information flashed across the screen. There were four hits!

She clicked on the first one. It was a report from the agency of Missing and Exploited Children. Stuart Samuels was a 6-year-old child from New Orleans who had been kidnapped by his biological father two years earlier. Jenny murmured a quick prayer for his safety. It was always difficult when children were in trouble.

The second Stuart Samuels was a black male born in 1917 who had wandered away from a nursing home in Memphis, Ten-

The Transient

nessee, the month before. She shook her head sadly, hoping against hope that he would be found soon so that the family could have closure. At this age, she was realistic enough to understand that his chances of survival outside the protective environment of a nursing home were slim and none.

Her hand began to shake as she moved to the third one. Her options were quickly being depleted. As the next profile flashed on the screen, she sat there staring at it breathlessly. Her heart was pounding as she leaned closer and stared carefully at the report. White male, born in 1955, missing since 1985 from Boise, Idaho. What really held her attention, however, was the picture. It was a 2 x 3 likeness in the lower right hand corner and it *could* be their Mr. Samuels. It was difficult to know for sure because his face was fuller, his hair darker and thicker, and he was smiling.

She looked up at the Lieutenant standing at her shoulder. "What do you think?"

He smiled, raising his right thumb in affirmation. "Go ahead and make the call," he directed kindly.

Soon she was on the phone to the Boise Police Department. After a five minute conversation, she was armed with the phone numbers of a sister and an uncle. She had asked the Boise Sergeant not to contact the family yet. She wanted to be sure he was still in town before notifying them.

She stood in the line at the night shelter, serving food and nervously straining to see down the line of hungry humanity, longing to see Stuart Samuels. She finally spotted him, caught his eye and smiled warmly. He responded to her friendliness and felt somewhat humbled by her friendly acceptance.

After serving all the meals, she moved to Mr. Samuels' table with a coffee pot. As she refilled cups at his table, she chatted with him.

TALES FROM THE SUNROOM

"How are you, Mr. Samuels?"

"Doing well, Ms. Roberts, and yourself?"

"I'm well, too. And I understand you've found a job. Will you be staying with us in Henson for awhile?" She was hopeful as she waited for his answer.

He was somewhat curious regarding her questions and her obvious interest in his plans. He felt no threat but was touched by her concern.

He smiled and replied, "Probably two or three more days. The supervisor asked me to stay until we complete the job we're on and I plan to."

"Will you be okay to stay here?" she inquired, indicating the shelter as his place of residence.

"Oh, yes ma'am. This suits me fine."

He noticed relief on her face, and she quickly got up and returned to the kitchen. She left the shelter a few minutes later after making certain everything had been taken care of and everyone had been fed.

Curious, he thought. Wonder what that was all about.

She rushed home, and called the number she had for a sister. She waited anxiously as the phone rang – once, twice, three times. Finally, a feminine hello.

"Hello?" she jumped to her feet. "Is this Emma Kinley?"

"Yes."

"Ms. Kinley, my name is Jenny Roberts, and I live in Henson, North Carolina. I work in the Records Division of our police department, and I don't want you to think that anything is wrong because it isn't, everything is fine, but do you have a brother named Stuart Samuels?" Her words flooded out all together in her excitement.

"Yes! Yes I do!" Emma Kinley's voice quavered with shock and disbelief.

The Transient

"I think, Ms. Kinley, that he's staying here at our local night shelter. He seems to be fine and has a job that will last for a couple more days, so I took a chance on calling you."

"But how?" Emma Kinley began.

Jenny understood her confusion and upcoming questions so she quickly told her how she had met Stuart, and where he was.

"I found him on the internet. I didn't have much information so I hope we're right. The picture on the site looks like Mr. Samuels but he's lost some weight and his hair is thinner."

"He's been gone for twelve years, Ms. Roberts," Emma explained, "so I'm certain there have been changes. I want to fly down there immediately and see for myself before he disappears again."

"I was hoping you would. Just call me back when you have your reservations made, and I'll pick you up, no matter what time. The nearest airport is Raleigh. We can talk because I'd really like to know what happened to bring him here. At the risk of sounding judgmental, he seems so intelligent and decent. Not the typical person we see on the street here in Henson."

"He is both, Jenny. And thank you for being so perceptive to those facts. I don't want to take time to get into the story now because I'm really anxious to make arrangements to get there. I've waited and prayed for this call for twelve years."

Within a half hour, Emma called Jenny with her travel arrangements. She would arrive at the Raleigh Airport at 5:04AM the next morning. Jenny assured her that she would be there. She then called Lt. Billings, updated him on what had happened, and told him she would take Emma by the shelter after picking her up in hopes of catching Stuart before he left for work. It would be close as the workers were picked up from the shelter by the temporary agency's van at 6:30AM. Henson was 40 minutes from the Raleigh Airport, so unless the plane was on time and there was no luggage to claim, they would miss him.

Jenny left for the airport the next morning at 4:00AM, and paced nervously until the 5:04 flight arrived, right on time. She watched as people filed out, straining to see a lone, middle-aged woman who was the keeper of Stuart Samuels' fate.

Jenny spied a distinguished looking lady with short, gray hair. She was tall like Stuart Samuels with the same intelligent eyes and strong jaw. She was slim and elegantly dressed in a black pantsuit trimmed in navy with a simple strand of pearls resting on her long neck.

Jenny approached her, and asked expectantly, "Are you Emma Kinley?"

"Yes, I am. And you're Jenny." Her face was covered with a warm smile, tinged with relief, nervousness and anxiety. She was carrying a small overnight bag and had no other luggage to retrieve. Jenny was encouraged by this, as she explained their tight time schedule.

"We need to get to the shelter before 6:30 in order to catch Mr. Samuels," she explained. "The van from the temporary agency arrives then to take the men to their jobs."

"It's very difficult for me to comprehend that Stuart is living in a night shelter and working for a temporary agency," Emma lamented as they hurried to Jenny's car. "He has always been the rock of stability and responsibility, the one all the family depended on in times of difficulty. He's the one with the levelheadedness and sensibility to undertake adversity and hardships, but when he lost his family, I'm afraid he lost himself."

Jenny noted that she was speaking of him in the present, so she had never given up hope of finding him. Please, let Mr. Samuels be her brother! Jenny pleaded silently.

"Here we are," she announced as she unlocked the car doors and helped Emma in with her bag.

The Transient

Soon they were on the highway and heading toward Henson. Traffic was still light this time of morning, and Jenny was grateful for yet another break.

"Stuart was a sociology professor at Central University in Boise," Emma began her story. "He was well known and respected around the country for his work with children of the ghetto. He was particularly intrigued by those he called the "untouchables" who grew up in horrendous surroundings, yet managed to live productive, law abiding lives. He was working on obtaining a grant to study this phenomenon when disaster struck.

"Stuart met Amy O'Connor in 1974. They met while they were both studying at Baylor University. All the family recognized at once that Stuart and Amy were soul mates, and they were perfectly matched to one another. It seemed that one knew what the other was thinking, and they would frequently say the same thing at precisely the same moment. It was quite uncanny. And very heartwarming!

"They married in 1979, right after Stuart obtained a position as professor at Central. They were so thrilled because Stuart was able to come back home. It wasn't long before he had become quite well known and respected within the academic community. He wrote prolifically for sociology publications, and within two years of his professorship, he had written a sociology textbook which was embraced by most of the major universities in the country."

"It sounds like you were very proud of him," Jenny interjected softly. Emma's devotion was obvious.

"Oh, my yes, Jenny. We all were. He's a very gifted person. Anyway, in 1982, little Stephanie was born. They were a beautiful family and were so happy. I remember that Amy used to say she felt guilty because they were so happy and blessed. As if it were too good to last. It turned out to be a

TALES FROM THE SUNROOM

very prophetic remark.

"When little Stephanie was 3 years old, she had a virus, and Amy was taking her to the doctor. A man in a pickup truck ran through a stop sign, and hit Amy's car on the driver's side. Stephanie was in a car seat behind Amy. He was going 55 when he hit them, and they were both killed instantly. The driver of the truck died the next day."

"Oh no," moaned Jenny, "I'm so sorry." No wonder his eyes are so sad, she thought.

"Well, needless to say, we were all devastated, and Stuart was inconsolable. In addition to my grief over Amy and Stephanie, I was terrified for him. His eyes were so dim and empty, just dead. It was as if the soul had been ripped out of him, and his body was still functioning on a superficial level.

"I begged him to come home with me as his despair was obvious, and stay a few weeks, but he refused. I never saw him again after we left the cemetery on the day of the funerals in 1985.

"The community was convinced he had committed suicide. None of his clothes were gone, and his car was parked by the side of the road near the interstate. All the lakes in the area were searched by divers, but nothing. We put signs up all over the state. People were wonderful, and in 1994, the FBI put him on the Internet's Missing Persons site. I was just sure we'd find him right away, and quite frankly, I had just about given up when you called."

She turned and looked kindly at Jenny, smiling slightly. She was impressed by Jenny's compassion.

They continued to chat as they traveled, sharing stories about their grandchildren, and Emma answering Jenny's questions regarding Stuart.

In what seemed like a very short time, Jenny exited off the

The Transient

highway onto Kline Drive and steered toward the night shelter.

"We'll be there in about five minutes." She glanced at the clock. It was 6:15. It was going to be close, but she thought they would just make it. Emma leaned forward, peering through the darkness, willing the car onward.

Jenny maneuvered the car into a parking space beside the shelter. The agency van was not in the parking lot so she felt certain they had made it. They exited and walked briskly through the early morning, their breaths making small, white puffs of fog as they moved. If she had not been in a hurry, Jenny would have played with these instant clouds. She enjoyed the fantasy of their brief existence, and related them to an attempt to catch a dream or a moonbeam. Her husband, Roger, had once built a tiny cage of wire mesh and presented it to her on their anniversary as a "fog catcher." They had enjoyed that moment tremendously.

They entered the shelter breathlessly, and Jenny anxiously scanned the small group of men standing near the back door. Her eyes stopped on Stuart Samuels, and she finally released the breath she was holding. She smiled and waved excitedly.

He saw her, smiled in response to her greeting, and then froze in place as he caught sight of the woman with Jenny. Confusion, shock, recognition and disbelief raced across his face as he realized that here was his sister, Emma.

Jenny suddenly became uneasy. He may have a heart attack, or he may be angry because Emma is here, or he may just walk away from both of us, she worried. Self-doubt pervaded her heart, and she wrung her hands together in distress as she waited for the scene to play out.

Stuart took a tentative step forward, held out his hand, and whispered, "Emma?"

Suddenly Emma was across the room, and threw her arms

around him joyfully.

"Oh, Stuart," she sobbed, "we've missed you so!"

He held her close, and as he raised his head to meet Jenny's gaze, his eyes, as were Jenny's, were filled with tears. It took several minutes for the scene to settle down so they could all communicate with some semblance of normalcy.

Words and questions and explanations and tears and laughter tumbled over each other as the drama unfolded. As soon as she could, Jenny offered to take them to her home for breakfast so they could talk, get re-acquainted, and make decisions.

She called Roger to let him know before he left for work. He made a fresh pot of coffee, picked up the newspaper, and placed the dog in her travel cage so she wouldn't bother their guests. He was used to surprise guests in their home, but having them for breakfast was a first. He was sorry he had to miss it!

Emma and Stuart talked animatedly all the way to Jenny's home and continued after arriving, as Jenny prepared bacon and pancakes for them all.

Stuart explained that the pain of all the memories was just too much for him after Amy and Stephanie died.

"It was worse than any physical pain I ever suffered. It was as if my heart had died, and there was no way that I could go back into that house and back into the classroom. I just allowed the darkness in my soul to swallow me.

"I thought about coming back in 1987, but I didn't know if I'd be welcomed or not. It was just easier to stay away. I guess I was a terrible coward, but I just didn't know where to turn or what to do. So I did nothing. After awhile, it became easier just to stay away."

"You're always welcomed back home, Stuart, but we all understood your grief and anguish. We hurt for you too, and were afraid that we'd never see you again. It was a scary, heartbreak-

The Transient

ing time for us all. I just regret that you spent so much terrifying time alone. But that's over now and you're going home."

Stuart hesitated, and both Emma and Jenny held their breaths. They waited for and dreaded his next statement.

"Emma...I'm not certain I can go back. There's nothing to go back to. I guess the house was foreclosed, I have no desire to teach anymore, even if I could after all these years, and Amy and Stephanie..."

"Yes, Stuart, they're still gone," Emma agreed, "and you have never let yourself grieve. You've carried this pain for twelve years, and it's time to face it. I don't mean to sound harsh, but you have more responsibility and character than to let your life end on the streets away from everyone who loves you. Amy wouldn't want that to happen."

Stuart cringed as the words stung his conscience, even though they were spoken with kindness and love.

"As far as your house is concerned, the courts granted me Power of Attorney after you disappeared, and I sold it along with all the furniture and your car. The money was placed in a CD and it's yours, Stuart. I never gave up hope that we'd find you, so everything I did, I did with the thought that you'd be back and need it again. You can find another job, or you can just rest for awhile until you decide what to do. And I insist that you stay with me, at least until you get on your feet."

Stuart's eyes were red-rimmed as he digested everything that had happened over the past hour. It seemed like a dream, and he was afraid he would wake up to find that none of it had happened. He was overwhelmed by the love and support from Emma, and the care and concern of Jenny in finding her. There must be something to this computer craze after all!

He hesitated for a few more breathless moments as he considered the prospect of going back to Iowa. His grief had never

TALES FROM THE SUNROOM

been resolved, and the thought of opening old wounds was not pleasant. He didn't relish the negative consequences of his return as he weighed them in his mind. He was weary. Weary of being lonely and alone and homeless and hungry so much of the time. But on the other hand, Boise was where he had lost Amy and Stephanie, where they had died and were buried, where he had lived and loved and worked and been incredibly happy. Once when they were discussing their happiness, Amy had stated, "Accept it as a gift, be grateful, enjoy it and understand that life is both good and bad, happy and unhappy."

Funny, he thought. I wonder why that thought just entered my mind?

Just then, Emma asked, "What would Amy want you to do, Stuart?"

He knew the answer to that. He reached out his hand to Emma and whispered hoarsely, "Okay, Emma. I'd really like to try. But I don't know how well it'll work out. It's been a long time since I was a normal human being. But I won't make any promises. If I can't handle it or if it doesn't work out, I'll have to leave again. But I will promise you this – I won't go back out on the street. That life is becoming too dangerous, and I'm getting too old for it. Also, I don't want to hurt you or anyone else anymore by causing you to worry. I'm beginning to realize just how selfish I've been, and I hope you can forgive me."

Emma embraced him, admonishing gently, "No, Stuart, not selfish. We all understand, and I can't say how I would have reacted under similar circumstances, but the important thing is to go on from here. Your promise is appreciated and accepted, and I'm certain the whole family will do all we can to help you through your pain and transition. I assure you that everyone is anxious to have you back.

"It'll work out, Stuart. I'm certain of it. I really feel that it

The Transient

was the right time for you to pass through here and find Jenny. She's the one who cared enough to check your name on the Internet. It wasn't an accident, and I can't help but believe that it was fate. And who are we to ignore fate?" she teased lightheartedly.

Jenny stood on the sidelines, watching the struggle, well aware of the emotional turmoil Stuart was feeling with memories and emotions so long stifled colliding in his mind. Reaching his decision was not simple, and she understood the gravity of the situation.

Stuart and Emma left for home the following morning after promising Jenny to stay in touch and keep her advised of Stuart's well being. She hugged them both as they boarded the plane and shrugged off their offers of praise and appreciation.

"I see many people at the police department who are in various life situations," she explained, "but there was something special about Stuart which I recognized as soon as he walked in. I'm just glad that it turned out so well, and I just *know* that things are going to work out fine for both of you."

The days and weeks turned into months, and Jenny received an occasional letter or phone call from Emma regarding Stuart's progress. He had opened an antiques business, and was doing quite well with it. He had been warmly welcomed back in Boise by his family, old friends, and even strangers. He bought a small condominium, and settled quietly into his life. He had not, however, as far as Emma knew, visited the gravesites of Amy and Stephanie.

Jenny was disturbed by this revelation, but was certain Stuart would handle it as he felt able. It was good that no one seemed to be pressuring him. They demonstrated a remarkable acceptance of his spirit and integrity.

About eight months after they left North Carolina, Jenny received a call early one evening from Stuart. She was surprised and pleased to hear from him.

"Jenny, I wanted to let you know that today I was finally able to visit the graves of Amy and Stephanie. I wasn't sure how I'd be able to handle it, and I sat in the car for over an hour before mustering enough courage to get out and go over there, but I finally did. As soon as I saw their graves, I was surrounded with a tremendous feeling of peace. That space is just a memorial to them, and they're both gone to another dimension, away from pain and hurt, and more importantly, they're both fine. I felt a little ridiculous that it's taken so many years for me to realize and accept that."

"Oh, Stuart, I'm so glad. And don't be so hard on yourself. We're all only human, you know."

They chatted for awhile, promising to keep in touch, and then Jenny hung up. Somehow she knew she would probably not hear from Stuart and Emma again except for maybe a Christmas card. That, however, was further indication that all truly was well with Stuart and his life, and no further contact was needed nor expected.

Toby and Beau

Friendship gives for the sheer joy of the gift, asking no payment.

—g. gurley

He pulled his pocket watch out, and checked it as the clock in the church tower on the square struck one.

"Come on, Beau; let's go eat," he called, as he pulled himself out of his chair.

Soon he was stepping off the walkway, standing at the edge of the cobblestone street, waiting for two horse drawn carriages to pass. Beau sat patiently at his feet, his tiny bright eyes following the horses as they clopped by. He jumped to his feet, wagging his tail excitedly as Toby exchanged greetings with one of the drivers, but he did not move until Toby started across the street, signaling to Beau that it was safe to continue.

Toby pushed open the door to the Korner Kitchen, held it for Beau, then closed it behind them. Each head in the pub lifted, and each face was crossed with a smile as warm phrases greeted the duo. Several patrons leaned over to scratch behind Beau's ears, and Mazie came out from behind the counter with a small treat for her favorite customer. Al, the cook shouted an exuberant "'Ello", and threw a link of sausage in the pan for their tiny guest.

In 1856 London, no one objected to a small dog in a pub, especially one as well behaved as Beau. He had been a daily fixture at the establishment since Toby found him abandoned, cold and hungry, five years earlier. His brilliant black eyes were barely visible through the mass of hair exploding over his face, but even those thick curls could not hide the intelligence in that miniature frame, nor could they hide the love and devotion he had for Toby.

Each day for as long as most of them could remember, Toby McLauren had eaten lunch at the Korner Kitchen. He and his wife had been childless, and she had died fifteen years earlier after a five year illness. Toby was a giant of a man who had worked as a blacksmith until an accident with a wench severed his hand six years ago. He possessed a quiet and gentle dignity in sharp contrast to his muscular size. He would literally fill a door with his frame, yet nearly disappear after entering a room. His dignified unpretentiousness allowed him to enjoy his privacy without being reclusive. He was, however, quite approachable and deeply respected by his neighbors and fellow Londoners, who had known him both as a blacksmith and a friend.

Toby had been lonely following the death of his wife, and had thrown himself into his work. His metal fencework, stair rails, balusters, and decorative ironwork were widely accepted and prized by those fortunate enough to attain them. His greatest work, however, was a high, intricate fence enclosing the front of the two hundred year old cemetery just a few blocks from his small home and the Korner Kitchen. The thin rods of iron were twisted, bent and molded into beautiful, complex designs almost lacelike in their delicacy, but the design promised to exist timelessly as long as it was cared for. The most breathtaking section was the huge double gate covering the entrance to the three acre

Toby and Beau

site. It represented Toby's concept of the tree of life, and spread majestically to the top corners, with branches reaching and cascading thickly to the edges of the sides and leaping above the top frames, like fingers reaching for heaven in determination not to be confined within a frame. The massive textured trunk supporting the thick limbs and branches was split in half as the doors opened. Each door was twenty-five feet wide and caused people to shake their heads in wonder as to how something so substantial could stand so solidly and open so easily.

He had begun work on the project shortly before his wife's illness. It grew and evolved as her illness progressed and became a love letter to her spirit. After her death, he worked with even more dedication and purpose, and had completed the gate and five hundred feet across the front when he had his accident. The fence represented twelve years of imagination, planning and artistry.

The directors of the cemetery decided to complete the project with a stone wall connecting each end of Toby's fence so as to enclose the remaining property. The city was disappointed that his work was incomplete, but the thick, solid stones enhanced and complemented the airiness of the ironwork, and gave the cemetery a coziness and comfort which were non-existent before Toby's work had begun. It became a prestigious, as well as historic area, with people coming from near and far to view the beauty of the fence.

Each day after finishing their meal, the two would walk to the cemetery, and Toby would sit by his wife's grave, quietly reflecting, smoking his beloved pipe. Beau would lie under a huge marble coffin next to the gravesite. The coffin set on twenty-four inch high piers placed under each corner of the box. The epitaph read, "He thought he was a head above everyone else." Toby had chuckled the first time he saw it, but it became a very

TALES FROM THE SUNROOM

nice place for Beau to rest away from the weather and pesky insects which pervaded the city.

The two became fixtures in the area, and people derived great comfort from seeing them on their daily sojourn. Beau's loyalty to his master and Toby's devotion to his wife's memory were heartwarming. Their presence seemed to bring order and peace to the day.

It was a beautiful, bright day in early June. Even the normal smokey soot from countless chimneys was thinner that day. Mazie looked up as the tower clock in the church struck one.

"Toby and Beau will be 'ere soon," she observed.

Al reached over for a thick piece of ham he'd saved that morning. He received great pleasure in feeding the gentle little Beau. 'E'll like this, he thought, as he slapped it in the pan.

Time passed and Mazie became concerned.

"They should be 'ere by now." She couldn't hide her worry.

"Maybe they just got delayed." Al was trying to hide his own uneasiness.

Mazie waited a few minutes more, and then moved across the floor to peep anxiously out the door. No sign of them anywhere. An hour later, she could wait no longer. She removed her apron and announced, "I'm going looking for 'em."

Al shouted as she exited, "Wait up! I'll go with ya." He locked the door of the empty pub on his way out.

They knocked on the door of Toby's small house but received no answer. They knocked louder and Mazie called out. Beau barked from inside, and they exchanged a brief glance before Al forced the door open.

Beau met them in the hall, barking anxiously, and ran to the back of the house. They followed and before they could get there, he ran back to them, barking insistently and impatiently.

"Awright, awright, old boy, we're coming!"

Toby and Beau

As they entered the dark bedroom, Mazie scooped Beau up and held him close. Al checked the motionless form on the bed, and shook his head sadly at Mazie.

"Oh, no!" she moaned, and buried her face in Beau's trembling fur.

She took him home with her, determined to care for him just as Toby had. He cried pathetically, pacing endlessly before the door of her flat, begging to be released. She took him out on a leash as she feared he would run away to Toby's home, and be injured in some way. She tied him to a bench in the pub while she worked. He would leap up, wiggling exuberantly each time the door opened, but would lie down in deep disappointment when Toby didn't enter.

The day of the funeral arrived, and Toby was laid to rest beside his beautiful Harriet. The gates he so lovingly created opened, and Toby entered for the last time. Beau trotted beside the casket and lay by it as the services were conducted. When it was time to leave, he refused to go. Mazie managed to capture him and carry him back to the pub.

As she entered, Beau wriggled free, and fled out the door. She bolted after him but was no match for his determination as he escaped. She found him lying on top of Toby's grave.

"Okay, little fellow," she stated kindly. "I understand. This is where you need to be right now so just stay. I'll keep an eye on you and make sure you don't go 'ungry."

The tower clock struck one that afternoon and Mazie looked up out of habit, then sadly realized her error. She went back to her chores and stopped when she heard a familiar bark at the door. Beau bounded in when she opened it, and was soon eating ravenously. He had refused to eat until now and was quite hungry.

As soon as he finished, he returned to the door, and looked up imploringly at Mazie. She smiled resignedly, opened the door

TALES FROM THE SUNROOM

and released Toby's tiny guardian. He rushed out, and she was certain he would return to the cemetery. Just to reassure herself, she stopped by that evening on her way home from work, and sure enough, there he was. He raised his head and wagged his tail briefly but made no effort to move from his sentinel spot. She placed a small bowl of water under the stilted marble casket near Toby's grave, turned to go, and blew Beau a kiss.

"G'night, Beau. See you tomorrow?"

Beau's bright eyes followed her as she left, then he dropped his head between his front paws and settled down for the night.

Each day shortly after the 1:00 tower clock's announcement, Beau would return to the Korner Kitchen for his one meal of the day. Immediately upon completing his repast, he returned to his master in the cemetery. Just as faithfully, Mazie would take fresh water to Beau daily, and when winter arrived, she placed warm hay beside the water hoping to entice him to leave his hallowed spot to escape the cold. She was encouraged when she found him between the stilts under the casket several cold afternoons.

Winter passed, then another and another. Three years after Toby's death, Harvey Gray, a new director, arrived at the cemetery. He was young with very modern and conservative views. He was appalled by Beau's presence, and immediately attempted to chase him away. Beau, however, was having no part of it, and Director Gray chased him for several hours on that first day he became aware that Beau was an unwelcomed resident. They ran in and out, around and behind the many monuments. Gray caught his toe on a partially submerged foot stone and fell sprawling across the graves. He scrambled up, cursing and fuming, while Beau scooted under a thick hedge for safety.

Gray lost sight of Beau when he fell and spent several minutes searching for the little guard, finally deciding he had suc-

Toby and Beau

ceeded in chasing him away. He limped off, rubbing his knee, muttering under his breath about the filthy beast who had invaded *his* cemetery.

Mazie was alarmed that evening as she arrived, and discovered that Beau was not at his usual spot on the grave or under the casket nearby. She called him softly, and soon heard a rustling in the bushes. Beau slipped out, wriggling happily at her feet.

"What's the matter, fella? Huh? Are you okay?" She soothed him as she rubbed his ears.

For several days, she discovered him in a similar state. She worried about him and mentioned her concern to Mitchell, the police Bobby in their area, as he was eating there one noon. Beau arrived for his meal while Mitchell was still there. Mazie approached him, rubbing his ears as she always did. He flinched and drew back from her touch.

"What's that?" she questioned as her hand touched something hard on his head. She checked and discovered dried blood on a small cut.

"Mitchell, it's blood!" Mazie was visibly shaken.

"Go ahead and feed 'im, Mazie, and I'll follow him when he leaves. Something's afoot."

Mitchell followed him from the pub. Beau stopped at the gate, glanced furtively about, and then dashed into the cemetery, darting behind stones and peeking out nervously before advancing to the next one, until he made his way to his beloved destination.

Strange, thought Mitchell. He acts like someone's chasing him.

Mitchell stood back out of sight and quietly watched. Shortly, he heard a shout and Beau leaped up, scampering away. Harvey Gray appeared, a large stick in his hand, and began to chase Beau.

TALES FROM THE SUNROOM

"'Ey, there, what are you doing?" demanded Mitchell.

Gray stopped short, obviously startled. As he saw the Bobby, he dropped the stick and began to sputter in confusion.

"That dog has no business here, and I won't have him in my cemetery!"

Mitchell moved toward him slowly, and spoke softly but with authority. "'E was here before you were, Mr. Gray, and 'e's doing nobody no 'arm. I'm warning you to leave 'im alone. If anything happens to him, I'll hold you personally responsible. And you don't want to deal with the good folks of this community if you hurt ole Beau."

"We'll just see about that," Gray sputtered. "I'll let the directors know 'e's here and they'll get rid of 'im, I'll wager. I was trying to be kind and run 'im off but the board may not be so charitable."

"Well, in the meantime, you've been warned not to harm the little bugger."

Mitchell stayed until Gray stormed off, and Beau came out of hiding. He comforted the little dog, and then he returned to the pub to make a report to Mazie.

She was livid and immediately began plotting her strategy to fight Harvey Gray. Fortunately, Al served on the board of directors at the cemetery so she knew she and Beau had at least one ally. He soothed Mazie as he promised to do all he could. He did share with her that none of the board members had ever complained or received a complaint that he knew of against Beau's being in the cemetery. Actually, several members had verbally praised the little dog for his loyalty and dedication. They found it both inspiring and touching in a sometimes cold, unfriendly world.

At Harvey Gray's request, a special meeting of the board was called within the week. He strode arrogantly, confidently into

Toby and Beau

the room and was met with cold, hard stares from the board as well as several angry citizens. These stares immediately took some of the starch out of his sails. Within thirty minutes of his entrance, he sat angrily trembling, flushed and drymouthed, before the group. They were firm and staunch in their decree that Beau stay at his chosen assignment.

He leapt up and cried passionately, "Either that dog goes or I do!"

He was met with stoney silence, and felt the color drain from his face as he realized what had just happened. He struggled to regain a degree of dignity before making a hasty retreat.

"Let's remember this when we get a new director," Al reminded. "We'll tell 'im that Beau stays."

The room erupted in applause and happy shouts. Mazie was particularly relieved and grateful to all the board, especially Al.

And so it was that Beau did stay for six more years. He began moving very slowly, his once bright eyes clouded with cataracts, and he took longer to arrive for lunch than he had in the past, but all the neighborhood kept an eye on him so that he was able to cross the street safely. Mazie visited him each and every evening with a gentle pat and kind word. Beau was quite the hero.

The inevitable day came when the fifteen year old dog didn't appear for lunch. Mazie looked up and met Al's eye. Neither spoke as she slipped her scarf over her head and exited the pub. Al removed his apron, following close behind her. Soon a small, sad group gathered behind them as they all moved toward the McLauren Memorial Cemetery.

Mazie gently picked up the tiny body lying on top of his master's plot, burying her tearful face in his graying curls. The men removed their hats and the women wept into their handkerchiefs.

TALES FROM THE SUNROOM

Two days later a large crowd gathered at Toby's gravesite. The priest at the tower church officiated as they prepared to scatter Beau's ashes over Toby's grave. Mazie and Al could not bring themselves to bury him away from this site, and even the compassionate board of directors couldn't grant permission to bury him here.

They waited silently for the church clock to strike one, as Mazie had requested. As it did, Father Rogers spoke of Beau's loyalty and faithfulness.

"Beau possessed attributes elusive to most humans. He was more than a friend – he became a guardian angel. He entered Toby McLauren's life at the depth of human grief and loneliness, and remained by his master's side, even after Toby's death. Beau was on earth a scant fifteen years, but he has touched many as few humans living much longer are able to do. He is now with his beloved friend, and they will be together forever. Rest well, thou true and loving servant."

After those few brief, eloquent words, Mazie lovingly scattered Beau's ashes over Toby's grave and stepped away. Each mourner tossed flowers on the spot – some had one or two and others had bouquets. Soon the area was covered with colorful offerings. It eased their pain and celebrated little Beau's existence among them. He had made a difference in their world.

Several months later, a local budding sculptor who had befriended Beau, pulled a wagon with a large, covered package into the pub and presented it to Mazie.

"I'd like for you to have this in memory of Beau. It seems tragic that he was so important to this community for there not to be something to mark his passage through our lives."

He removed the canvas covering, and there was a beautiful, black marble statue of Beau gazing back at them. His curls wound and cascaded down the figure and over his face. His tiny eyes appeared almost bright and sharp, even though they were of stone. His mouth was open in an enthusiastic breath with his tiny tongue furled out excitedly, and he was perched on his hind legs, as he did while at Toby's feet.

"Oh, William," Mazie gasped emotionally, "it's lovely! 'E looks so real!"

Her obvious pleasure and gratitude warmed him, and made him glad that he had created this work. The little creature had mattered, and now all of time would know.

The statue set in a place of honor until Al and Mazie were able to get permission to place it on a pedestal, at the head of Toby's grave.

"'E'll be here forever, with his good friend, Toby," Al decreed as they set the figure in place.

Daughter of the Mountain

Kindness shared is heaven's art that softens life and warms the heart.
                                                        —unknown

Kate walked up the dusty road winding through the tall red, yellow, orange and brown adorned trees. The sun was bright and clear, the air crisp with early fall's bite. Today was more of a nibble than a bite, however, and she was enjoying the warmth of the sun on her shoulders. The falling leaves would occasionally strike her as she walked, and she could hear the rustle of woodland creatures in the woods on either side of the dirt road.

The sun glinted off her auburn hair, causing it to sparkle with chips of copper and gold. It was long and thick and rested effortlessly on her shoulders. Her gait was slow and somewhat labored as she maneuvered her swollen body over the ruts and bumps. Her baby was due in six weeks, and she knew that the new child and the harsh mountain winter would prevent her from taking her long, meditative walks, so she relished each step along this beloved and familiar route.

She approached the small cottage tucked far into the woods on the right, and instinctively turned her gaze toward it. For as long as she could remember, she had been enthralled by the enchantment of the small log dwelling, and mystified by the reclusive old gentleman who lived there. She would sometimes see Edward Thomas out in the yard or on his porch, and had even seen him in town from time to time at the general store. She would always smile and wave, or speak, if she was close enough, but he seldom responded. He would just watch her with a deep, enduring pain in his eyes which never failed to tug at her heart. She would wonder what caused his pain and his aloofness. He never frightened her as he did so many of her friends, because she saw no anger or malice in him – only the pain and sadness from deep within his soul.

She stopped outside the split rail fence by the side of the road and gazed down the drive toward his house. She noted the ever-present bird feeders, two of which had squirrels for guests, even though there was a small platform erected further over in the yard which contained ears of dried corn. It was obviously there for the squirrels, but they were more interested in the contents of the bird feeders at the moment. Salt licks were stationed at the edges of the woods as a gift to the forest deer. She marveled at his obvious kindness to the woodland creatures, and could feel no fear or animosity toward him.

Some of the local boys had in the past delighted in making him the brunt of their pranks. They would pull a section of split rail fence down or tear his mailbox down. They would toss watermelons, tomatoes or pumpkins from their car into his driveway throughout the year, and then speed away as quickly as possible on the dirt road, laughing noisily, feeling quite brave and proud of themselves. Kate saw them as cowards and was never shy about telling them so. Her chastisement would humble them briefly, because Kate was not only the prettiest girl on the mountain, but she was also the most outspoken. Her green eyes would flash like flint rock when she was angry. The sting of her anger would soon dissipate, and their relatively harmless delinquency would resume. They did, however, eventually outgrow their antics and left the old man alone. The newer generation of youth had little interest in the mystery of the old man. They preferred to gather in the lights of the small village around the local bowling alley or hamburger hangout, and dream of escaping their tiny town rather than wander over the bumpy, difficult to maneuver dirt roads to harass a harmless gentleman.

Kate, on the other hand, remained loyal to her feelings of compassion for Mr. Thomas. Once when she was still in high school, she mustered enough courage to take some persimmon pudding to his front door as a gift of friendship. She loved the sweetness, and somewhat meaty texture, of these wonderful fall fruits and looked forward to the first frost each autumn so they would fall from the trees to be retrieved for her beloved dessert. She had to arrive early to retrieve them as they were also favorites of the deer, raccoons and 'possums. They were soft and sticky as she gathered them, and she was not particularly fond of their taste when she licked her fingers, but when mixed with flour and sugar and eggs and spices and sweet potatoes, persimmons were sheer ambrosia.

As she approached the cottage door on that first time with her offering, she heard the babbling of a mountain spring. She looked to her left and saw it dancing down the gentle slope of the yard. She couldn't detect its origin but knew it wasn't far away. She walked quietly across the front porch. There was an old porch swing hanging at one end, a barrel filled with pine cones to kindle the fireplace, a small stack of firewood near the door, and a ladderback chair backed up against the wall of the house. A small chipmunk scurried away as she stepped onto the porch.

TALES FROM THE SUNROOM

She held the plate of persimmon pudding, wrapped carefully in aluminum foil, and knocked lightly. There was no answer. She knocked again, this time just a bit louder. Still no answer. She set the gift down on the ladderback chair and quietly retreated.

As she later returned from her walk up the mountain, she noticed that the plate was gone from the chair. She smiled and skipped down the road toward home.

Through the years, she would periodically leave small treasures for Mr. Thomas. Sometimes it was a small jar of apple jelly, or a mason jar filled with her father's famous scuppernong wine, or even pecans she picked up from beneath the large pecan tree which grew in the field behind their home. She also left bouquets of daisies, or goldenrods or Queen Ann's lace bundled together for him. She quit waiting for Mr. Thomas to answer the door, and would just knock, leave her gift and go away. But he did begin nodding to her or waving briefly when she caught him outside.

Kate graduated from high school, and soon afterward, she married Tommy Benton. He had graduated four years earlier, had joined the Army and was now back home in Woodland, North Carolina. Many of the young people still in high school were surprised when he returned. They promised themselves if they ever got away, they'd never be back. Tommy smiled wisely as they related this determination to him. He didn't bother to tell them that he had felt the same way several years ago, but after four years away from the sanctuary of the mountain, and the love of his hometown, he was grateful to return. And now he had captured the heart of the beautiful and feisty Kate Davis. He was blessed.

They moved into a small house about a mile and a half from Mr. Thomas. She continued her long walks, and her small gifts to him.

On their first Thanksgiving after marrying, Kate cooked a large traditional turkey dinner for their families. Both their parents came as well as Kate's sister, her husband, and Tommy's three brothers. The men gathered in the yard after the feast and were talking and laughing when Kate came out, carrying a large brown bag.

"What's that?" Tommy inquired.

"Lunch for Mr. Thomas," she explained.

Tommy smiled gently and said, "Be careful. Do you want me to go with you?"

"No, I'm fine. I'll be back soon."

The brothers laughingly recounted their mischievous acts against Mr. Thomas when they were growing up, and also recalled Kate's scoldings. They used to hide in the woods, and watch to make certain Mr. Thomas was either in bed or gone to town before doing their mischief. Facing the wrath of Kate was not nearly so threatening as the fear of facing Mr. Thomas.

As she left the meal and turned to leave, Kate heard the door behind her open. She turned and saw Mr. Thomas standing there.

"Hello, Mr. Thomas. I'm Kate Benton, and I wanted to share the first Thanksgiving meal I've ever cooked by myself with you." There was pride in her voice as she spoke.

"I know who you are, girl," he smiled slightly. That same age-old pain was in his eyes, but there was a gentle softness on his face and in his voice.

"Happy Thanksgiving, Mr. Thomas," she smiled as she turned to leave.

"Happy Thanksgiving, girl."

Kate's thoughts returned to the present, away from the Thanksgiving last year, as she moved from his driveway to return home. She could not see him standing behind his window, watching her quietly as she walked away. He left the window and stepped out the back door. His eyes traveled to a clearing about fifty yards away. He walked slowly to the clearing, knelt before the two graves, and gently brushed the fallen leaves away.

Mary Thomas, Beloved Wife, 1942-1963
Michele Thomas, Infant Daughter, 1963

That was Kate's last walk before the birth of their son, David Christopher. He was two weeks early, and was born two days before Christmas. When she went into labor early, Tommy nervously teased her that if he was born on Christmas, they were going to name him Santa Rudolph. Kate laughed in spite of her pain and retorted, "Well, we'll just see about that, Tommy Benton!" He smiled at her high spiritedness, even when she was in pain. That was one of the many things he loved about his Kate.

He placed her in the car after notifying her parents, and drove carefully toward the hospital, aware of every bump and hole in the road. She reached over and gently touched his arm as she saw the concern and strain in his demeanor. She was soothed by his attempts to dodge the potholes, and ease around the sharp curves of the narrow mountain road.

Tommy pulled into a parking place outside the emergency room, leaping out of the car almost before it stopped rolling.

"I'll be right back, baby," he promised as he ran through the double doors into the hospital.

In a few seconds, he returned with an armada of nurses, aides, a security guard and a wheelchair. They quickly transported Kate inside and began working with her. Her blood pressure was fine, there was no fever, and she was in full labor with delivery imminent. Dr. Foster was quickly called and advised of her vitals.

"She's a couple of weeks early but it looks like the baby's coming anyway. I'll be there shortly."

Kate's parents arrived and her mother rushed to her side before they wheeled her into delivery.

"Are you okay, sweetheart?" she asked anxiously.

"No-o-o-o-o!" moaned Kate, "I'm not. It hurts like fury!"

"It'll be over soon, sweety," she soothed. "Do you want Tommy in here?"

"Not now!" gasped Kate through her pain. "This is his fault, and he'd do well to stay away from me right now!" Kate screamed out in pain and pulled herself up on the rails of the bed in her attempt to escape the contractions.

The nurse rolled her over gently and administered a spinal block, muttering to herself that Dr. Foster should have ordered this the first time they called him. Kate didn't even notice what was happening through the haze of her agony, but shortly she began to feel blessed relief.

"There's a young man out here who's very anxious to see you, Kate," explained a nurse.

Kate felt somewhat more charitable toward Tommy since her pain had eased so she smiled, "Let him in."

"Are you okay, baby?" he implored. He looked terrified and Kate was touched by his concern.

"The pain's better now, Tommy, and I'll be fine. I just want to get this over with. Don't worry, this is normal and something I have to get through. He'll be here soon and then I can rest."

In a few minutes, Dr. Foster arrived, checked Kate, and ordered her into the delivery room. "I see the baby's head," he announced. "It's almost over, honey," he soothed Kate.

"I'm fine now, doctor. The pain is almost gone, but where were you awhile ago?"

He laughed as he pulled on his gloves and administered orders to the attendants. Kate gave two short pushes, and it was over. She heard the first cry of her son, and tears of joy escaped her eyes.

"Congratulations, Kate. You have a beautiful baby boy. He's a little small but he looks like he has all his parts."

They laid him on her chest, and she smiled happily as she counted all his fingers and toes. Ten and ten. His indignant bellow told them his lungs were fine.

"It's a good think he only has one mouth," Kate giggled.

"Yep, there's nothing wrong with his lungs," Dr. Foster stated. "He weighs five pounds, four ounces but that's okay. We're going to have him checked out by the pediatrician now, so we'll bring him to you later. You need to rest, and his daddy and grandparents are anxious to see him."

Kate was drifting off to sleep in her room later when Tommy came in.

"Baby, he's beautiful," Tommy breathed. His eyes were moist with emotion.

Kate smiled, a deep sense of satisfaction flooding through her. She burrowed deeper into the warmth of the bed and prepared to drift away.

"His name is David Christopher," she stated sleepily. "Oh, and Tommy, don't forget to take Christmas lunch to Mr. Thomas. And there's a present for him under the tree. I crocheted a scarf for him."

"Okay, baby," he smiled. Even after what she had been through, she was still thinking of others. "I'll take care of it. You just rest now, Mommy."

Mommy. What a beautiful word!

The weeks sped by as Kate and Tommy settled into being new parents. The diapers, formula, middle of the night feedings, mountains of laundry, and bathtime all combined to make the days and nights short and hectic.

Daughter of the Mountain

"I can't believe how much work there is for just one little baby," Kate lamented to her mother over the phone one morning. She caught a glimpse of herself in the mirror as she folded clothes. She had quickly learned to busy her hands as she talked on the phone so as not to waste one precious moment.

She was shocked by the reflection staring back at her from the mirror.

"Mom, I look terrible," she cried. "I have steamer trunks under my eyes, and my hair looks like something's been sucking on it!"

Sarah Davis chuckled at her daughter's colorful description.

"You're just tired, honey. I'm coming over after supper to spend the night so you can sleep. On second thought, I'll bring supper over there, and your dad can go back home after. That way you won't have to cook."

"Oh, thank you, Mom," she gushed. "That'll be wonderful!"

Kate felt better just knowing that relief was on its way, and hummed softly as she finished folding clothes. She was interrupted by a light tapping at the door.

She frowned at the interruption and moved impatiently to the door. It better not be a salesman, she thought.

She opened the door, and was stunned to see Mr. Thomas standing there. She stared at him speechlessly for several seconds before regaining her composure.

Finally, she smiled warmly and said, "Why, Mr. Thomas! What a wonderful surprise. Please – come in!" She stepped aside and held the door open widely.

He thrust a small, handcarved wooden horse toward Kate, and spoke self-consciously, "This is for the baby."

"His name is David Christopher. Please come in to see him," she implored as she took the gift. "You made this yourself, didn't you, Mr. Thomas?"

TALES FROM THE SUNROOM

Edward Thomas became a frequent visitor in the Benton's home. He was accepted and welcomed as a family member. There was never any question about his acceptance and importance to the family, especially to Kate. Her persistent, patient kindness had awakened his natural love and goodness which had been dormant since the death of his wife and daughter on the day little Michele was born over 30 years before. Kate's undying loyalty had gradually broken down the wall of pain and anger he had hidden behind for so long. This spirited, loving daughter of the mountain was now an integral part of his happiness and joy.

Kate's Persimmon Pudding
2 cups persimmon pulp, pressed through a colander to remove pits
2 cups sugar
½ cup melted butter
½ teaspoon soda
2 cups coarsely grated, raw sweet potato
1 ½ cups plain flour
2 cups milk
2 eggs
1 teaspoon ground cinnamon
1 teaspoon vanilla flavoring

Mix flour, sugar, spice; add milk, persimmon and eggs. Mix thoroughly by hand. Add vanilla and butter, then add sweet potato. Butter 8x13" pan and pour mixture in. Bake at 350 degrees about an hour or until set in the middle. Cool before cutting into squares.

Connected

It is not the differences, but the responses to these differences that make us human.
—unknown

Sahndo peeked through the leaves of the lush underbrush surrounding the small clearing. There was no game present, and his disappointment coupled with his exhaustion caused him to drop his head dejectedly.

He moved carefully out of the covering, more from habit than necessity, as hunting had made being stealthy second nature. He slipped the quiver of arrows off his shoulder, placed it along with his bow on top of a large boulder centered in the clearing, leaned his spear against the side, pulled himself up and sat there resting and contemplating. The rock maintained the warmth of the sun, which it had absorbed during the day, and Sahndo rested comfortably.

He was hunting alone today as it was not yet the season for the men to travel across the plain in search of big game for the winter. The new generation of life in the plain had not yet left their mothers. The young birds had left the nests, so it would be another two moon changes before the men would leave their huts and their families to hunt for the winter store. They would travel from their village by the lake, through the woods, crossing the rocky plain to this oasis. Beyond this pond area, a ridge of high rocky hills would be ascended, and on the other side lay the grassy plains filled with herds of large animals. Smaller game populated the immediate area surrounding the village.

He retreated briefly into the past as he remembered former hunts. Big game of a bear or antelope or even a mammoth would be brought back to the lake people's settlement, and there would be an explosion of activity, and urgent animation as the meat was prepared for nourishment during the coming winter. The women and children stripped, cleaned and butchered the meat while the men salted and smoked it in a special smokehouse set in the center of the other shelters so as to help protect it from scavengers and wandering carnivores.

Long ago, the builders had discovered that by building the smokehouse of mud bricks, the fire and smoke inside hardened these blocks, making the building quite permanent. Their huts were constructed of poles, limbs, grasses and other available materials so as to make them portable as they changed the location of their settlement.

There was very little sleeping for any of the population during the many days it took to cure and guard the meat, and process the hides. Most of their diet during the warm season consisted of smaller game such as birds, fish and small mammals, as well as roots, berries, nuts and vegetables raised in their garden. But when the cold arrived, the group united in their goal to survive. It was an invigorating, exciting time, this annual hunt, but the underlying urgency of survival did not escape the purpose of this activity. They also smoked fish while the meat cured to help ensure variety in their winter diet.

The lake people were living at the dawn of man in a hostile, dangerous world. There was no written language, few tools, little

Connected

aid during illness or injury, and infrequent contact outside their own group. They remained largely isolated from what lay beyond their lake and the plain . They moved short distances around the lake from time to time, as they needed fresh land. They had learned that crops would not always thrive in the same ground. Also, their waste and garbage became overwhelming after several cold seasons. They moved at the end of five winters, marking the winters by creating a rock altar at the end of each, and when they had five tables, a group of men sought a new site on the lakeshore. They had no recorded history to indicate their age, but knew their people were ancient, as they frequently had to tear down existing remains of altars at a new site so as to begin the cycle again. Their lake was vast and required a period of fourteen sunrises to circle.

Sahndo lived with his father, Monda, and mother, Auva. He remembered two moves with his people during his lifetime, and last year had been his first time with the fall hunt. The men had killed a young mammoth, and it had taken five days to return it to the settlement. They hastily butchered and salted it in the field so as to transport it, and the women finished the work back at the village.

Sahndo was hoping to bring home a large kill today—not only to feed his village, but to receive the status of passing from childhood to manhood. The first solo kill was a rite of passage practiced by his people for longer than any of them knew.

As his mind focused on his ambitions and hopeful goal, he suddenly was alerted by a splashing in the pond behind a grove of trees beyond his clearing. He immediately grasped his spear and bow, tossing his quiver of arrows over his shoulder, while sliding swiftly and silently off his rock. This could be the quarry he was seeking. The splashing was neither reckless nor careless, but was intense enough to be made by a larger creature than a beaver, duck, or some other small game.

He crept stealthily, warily through the brush, his muscles tense, his senses alert. The thickness of the growth hid him from sight but also blocked his view of the pond. He carefully, slowly pulled aside the leaves so as to peer cautiously in the direction of the splashing. As his eyes focused on the source of the disturbance, he stopped in shock, his breath caught in his throat, his heart racing.

It was a man of the caves standing in the pond, the water reaching his knees. He was bent over, his hands extended to the surface, looking as though he was trying to see through the water. He appeared to be about the same age as Sahndo, but he was larger. His hair was shaggy, thick and matted with tight curls, and he had the beginnings of a full beard. In contrast, Sahndo had light brown, straight hair with just a little fuzz on his cheeks, and he was much smaller in stature with arms and legs which appeared almost emaciated in comparison to this caveman.

The lake people hated and feared the cave people. Sahndo did not know the reason for this fear and hatred, but he frequently heard men around the fires telling of hunting and killing these creatures if they wandered too close to the village. Sahndo had never known it to happen, but some of the lake people told tales of children being carried off and eaten by these cave dwellers.

Sahndo felt cold chills as the muscles in his arms and legs tightened, his mouth became dry and his pupils dilated. He gripped his spear as he decided which weapon would better serve to kill this disgusting beast. He decided the bow and arrow would be more accurate at this distance. He gently, slowly leaned the spear against the trees, quietly returned the misplaced branches to their original position, and removed an arrow to place in his bow. He maneuvered carefully so as not to disturb his surroundings. He needed to gain a vantage point to view his target.

Connected

He pulled the bow back slowly and deliberately, feeling the tension in the bowstring as it tightened. Suddenly, the caveman lurched forward, grasped at something under the water, and tossed it on the shore in one smooth, fluid motion. Sahndo was temporarily caught off guard by this apparent agility. He had always believed that cave people were clumsy and bulky, barely able to walk upright.

A large fish landed unceremoniously on the shore where it had been tossed. The caveman quickly descended on his catch, thrusting a large stone knife into the frantic creature. As the fluttering and leaping ceased, joyful laughter escaped from the lips of the fisherman. Once more, Sahndo was shocked. This was a happy sound, very similar to the sounds the lake people made. And he killed the fish with a weapon! Sahndo had no idea that they had knives. He visualized them with crude clubs and simple rocks.

He remained behind the leaves watching, eager to see what else this strange, frightening man-creature would accomplish. He nearly fell through the branches as this awkward looking man kept spinning a stick on a base of what appeared to be leaves and similar debris, until a small column of smoke floated into the air. He knelt over, blowing gently, and suddenly, a small flame erupted. Sahndo gasped aloud, clasping his hand over his mouth to ensure his presence was not discovered.

The lake people had captured fire from a burning forest many years ago and guarded it with their very lives. It gave them warmth, comfort and safety from wild animal attacks as well as cooked their food, so it was their life source. Two men were posted around the fire each and every night to guard and feed it. During the day, the women tended it while the men hunted and fished. There were many fires in the settlement, but the mother fire was covered by a shelter of mud bricks cut from the lake's edge. It was similar in construction to the smokehouse but much smaller. The fire-baked bricks made the shelter nearly impervious to weather. This magic from the hands of the caveman was incomprehensible, and Sahndo doubted his own eyes. Perhaps the fire was stored somewhere that Sahndo could not view from this distance.

Soon the fire-making fisherman was eating his catch, hot from the coals of the impossible flames. He ate his fill, wrapping the leftovers in large green leaves, binding with a thin vine, and placing the package carefully in an animal skin pouch by his side. He crouched on his heels by the fire, gazing unseeingly across the small pond, lost in his thoughts.

Sahndo no longer had any desire to kill this man creature. He felt strangely connected to him in a way that was beyond any feeling this young lake man had ever before experienced.

As his thoughts returned to his own position, he realized it was getting late, and he had a long distance to cover to get back to his village. He readied himself to retreat when a move by the caveman caused him to stop.

He stared in amazement and disbelief as this awkward, ugly creature leaned his head back. A long, wrenching cry of anguish, loneliness and grief rose from deep within his large chest. The sincerity of his agony chilled and touched Sahndo. His shaggy head fell forward as he buried his face on his knees. The caveman wept.

Sahndo moved quickly across the terrain, anxious to reach his village before the darkness overtook him. As he ran, his mind was filled with the wonders he had witnessed this day. Everything he had been taught by his people about the cave people was called into question, and he didn't know how to understand it. He decided to keep this newfound knowledge to himself. He also decided to return to the small pond in the forest to try and

Connected

learn more about this strange, confusing caveman.

As the last rays of daylight disappeared, he was forced to slow his pace, and pick his way precariously over the darkened space. He used his spear to identify rocks and crevices while keeping his senses tuned to the night sounds stirring around him. He was frightened.

He decided to seek shelter under a rock and await the sunrise. As he peered around, straining to see through the darkness, his eye caught sight of a faint glow in the distance. He watched it for a few minutes, and realized it was moving toward him. In a short time, the glow became individual, flickering balls of flame. It was torches. His people were searching for him! He sent forth an immense shout that echoed across the plains, sending unseen inhabitants fluttering and scampering.

The torches continued, and Sahndo moved forward with a new determination and hope. He stopped only to repeat his shouts. Finally, the lights stopped and seemed to be listening. He shouted with even more enthusiasm, laughing aloud with joy and relief as he heard faint shouts answering him. Soon he was in the embrace of Monda, surrounded by the laughing, back slapping men from the village.

Shortly, the smokey roofs of his village loomed ahead, and the shapes of many of the villagers not with the search party were outlined against the flickering light of campfires. Monda shouted the good news. "We have found Sahndo! He is well!"

A collective cry of relief rose from the group. One in particular was relieved. Auva clasped her hands together joyfully, and ran forward to greet her lost son.

"Where have you been, my son? I've been so afraid!" Her feigned anger could not hide her happiness.

Soon Sahndo was lying in the hut of his parents, his belly full and his heart happy to be home. He was reflecting once more

TALES FROM THE SUNROOM

on the events of the day, when he heard angry shouts coming across the compound. His mother sat up, reaching out to grasp Monda's arm in alarm and concern.

"Bruel is hurting his family again, Monda."

"Hush, woman. We cannot stop it. The council has warned Bruel, but it just made it worse on Kesa and Amik. Unless Kesa asks the council for protection against her mate, there is little that can be done."

"I worry about Amik. She will soon be ready to take a mate, and all the young men of our village are afraid of Bruel."

Bruel had been the village brute for all of his life. He would especially bully the smaller and weaker villagers, causing the council to call him forward for discipline. He was warned to cease his unprovoked attacks or risk expulsion from the village. Expulsion was likened to a death sentence as each member of the group depended on the other for survival. He had ceased his physical attacks, and his verbal insults were tolerated, but he became a social outcast.

Kesa's father had died, and her mother was ill so Kesa had no one to care for her. She was an only child as her two brothers had died in infancy. Bruel offered to take Kesa as a mate, and the council reluctantly agreed.

Soon after their marriage, Bruel began to abuse Kesa. She never complained, and struggled to please Bruel. She had been very close to delivering their first-born, and was heavy with child, moving slowly and clumsily. Bruel demanded that she bring him water one evening as they sat outside their hut. She struggled to get to her feet so as to comply, but moved too slowly for the impatient and cruel man. He lashed out viciously, knocking her to the ground. Several men jumped to her defense, and the women rushed to her side. Soon the tiny Amik was born, and Bruel was held captive by the council until they could decide his fate.

Connected

Kesa pleaded with the council on Bruel's behalf. He was all she and her daughter had, such as he was. The council reluctantly agreed to let Bruel stay, but he was warned that if he were seen striking his mate or child in an abusive manner, he would be expulsed. Since that day, he had kept his anger and abuse inside their hut. Kesa did not complain so the council could do nothing. Recently, however, the shouts and crashes had escalated. It was a source of great stress and pain for the entire village.

The shouting ceased, and soon Sahndo was deep in sleep, exhausted by the day's adventures. His dreams were filled with weeping cavemen, fire exploding from their fingers and tongues, men lost in mist and darkness, crying for and seeking their families. First it was Sahndo crying out for his people, and then the caveman was crying out. Could he be seeking his family? It didn't seem possible but the thought tortured Sahndo. He awoke tired and confused as he became aware of the comforting smell of Auva's breakfast, and the laughter of the lake children playing outside.

Each morning for the next seven sunrises, he returned to the pond and studied this strange being who had such a grip on his emotions. Auva worried about her son's strange behavior, but her concerns were dismissed by Monda.

"He's just getting ready to go on the big hunt, and is trying to make a catch before then." Monda assured his concerned wife.

On the eighth day, Sahndo crept up to his vantage point by the pond only to find the water empty. There was no caveman there, and he felt an immediate concern. He hoped the man had not been injured or was sick. Maybe he had just moved on.

Sahndo sat there for a few minutes, then slowly backed away to leave. As he did, he heard an almost indiscernible sound by a large tree. He whirled and was startled by the appearance of the caveman, watching Sahndo. He cried out in alarm, backed up, tripped over a fallen branch, and fell backward, striking his head on a tree stump. He was momentarily stunned as terror, regret and anger rushed through him.

I'm so sorry, Mother, Father... He was certain he was about to die at the hand of this hairy brute of a man looming over him.

But no attack was made. Instead the caveman showed concern for the fallen lake man, making no move of aggression or threat. He held his open hand out for Sahndo to grasp. Sahndo shook his head to clear his senses, rubbing the knot rising up from contact with the stump, then struggled to escape.

As he scrambled to his feet, he lost his balance once more, and fell on his hands and knees. He crawled away as quickly as he could, looking very much like a giant crab. His would-be rescuer laughed heartily.

Sahndo stopped at the sound of the laughter. There was no malice noted but simply glee in the hearty laugh. He rolled over, looked at his enemy and began to smile in spite of his fear and doubt. He stood, attempting to compose a portion of his dignity, placed his right hand on his chest and stated, "Sahndo."

The caveman appeared confused, so Sahndo repeated his greeting. His companion stood silently for a brief period, absorbing the meaning of this signal, then placed his right hand tentatively on his own chest. "Tog."

As the days passed, the two spent many hours communicating with words, gestures and signs. Sahndo learned that Tog's family had all been killed by the "hairless men." Sahndo's kind, though not his tribe, he realized with shame. Tog had run far away and was now completely alone. There were no caves nearby, and he was afraid to venture very far in search of one. He feared those men were still out there somewhere, and he had no protection against them.

Connected

Tog had been aware of Sahndo's presence for several days, and had even followed him to the edge of the woods, determining that Sahndo was alone and no immediate threat to him. He had no idea how long Sahndo had been watching him, but he was certain he could have been killed numerous times by the hidden lake man. Tog's loneliness and curiosity were stronger than his fear; thus he had risked approaching Sahndo so boldly and recklessly.

Sahndo explained that he was hunting when he found Tog, and had to have a kill for his village before the big fall hunt. Tog appeared alarmed when Sahndo stated he needed a big kill, but Sahndo quickly reassured him by stating the kill had to be meat they ate.

Early the next morning as Sahndo arrived at the pond, Tog motioned for him to follow. Before noon, Sahndo had killed a large panther under Tog's guidance. He was thrilled but also perplexed. Killing it was one thing, but how was he to get it back to the lake alone?

They soon constructed a litter of poles tied together, and loaded the carcass onto it. It was a cloudy, cool early fall day so Sahndo decided to return to the village before completing the butchering. They removed the internal organs to make it weigh less, but one whole piece was easier to control alone than numerous cuts. He looped the large vines attached to the front over his shoulders and pulled.

After much tugging, struggling and digging his feet into the ground, he managed to move his burden a few feet. He quickly realized he would never be able to get it across the rough region to his home.

He continued struggling, his muscles aching, lungs pumping and sweat building on his forehead. Suddenly, the load lightened, and he moved forward easily. He turned to see the reason

TALES FROM THE SUNROOM

for his relief, and observed Tog holding up the back of the litter. Sahndo objected but Tog pressed forward, forcing Sahndo to move on.

They stopped to rest, and Sahndo reminded Tog that it would be dark long before a return trip could be made to the pond. Also, Tog had no shelter against the night dangers. Even though the fall was young, light frosts were evident each morning, and the night without shelter would be most uncomfortable. The lake men were leaving for their annual hunt the next week, as the frosts were a signal that animals would be herding, and consequently, easier to locate. The cold kept the meat from spoiling so they were able to transport it over a longer distance and still have fresh meat. This was a welcomed break from the normal staple of smoked and dried meat.

Even though the cold was a gift from Mother Earth, which enhanced their diet, it was also a signal to prepare for the approaching bitter winter. They stayed close to their village and in their huts, leaving only to perform the normal duties of the village, such as guarding the mother fire and carrying in firewood. This knowledge of the cold made it difficult for Sahndo to think of leaving his friend stranded in the open.

Still Tog refused to leave his friend, even as he peered fearfully into their surroundings where they rested. He was searching for the hairless ones who killed his people, and was also uneasy about approaching Sahndo's village. The others may not be so tolerant of Tog. Sahndo was likewise distressed over the dilemma and felt responsible for Tog's plight.

When they caught sight of the first smokey haze from the village, Sahndo stopped. He looked around, trying to locate some semblance of shelter for Tog in the rocky surroundings. Suddenly he had an idea. They slipped behind some boulders, and Sahndo began stacking smaller stones in a mound under a ledge

Connected

that protruded from the large cluster. There was not enough space to stand but his friend would be safe from predators and frost through the night. Sahndo would bring him food the next morning and accompany him back to the pond.

Soon Tog was comfortably hidden from view, wrapped in Sahndo's fur wrap, his knife and club close by his side. Sahndo was uneasy and reluctant to leave him, but Tog motioned for him to go.

Sahndo struggled with his burden over the remaining distance, and was met by several of the village men as they noticed his approach. He was greeted with much adulation and joy. His first kill! And a very large quarry at that. The shaman blessed the kill, and declared it to be an omen of prosperity and plenty for the upcoming hunt.

The women descended on the panther and soon had the meat cut and distributed, with the largest and best portions along with the hide, given to the hunter as reward and recognition of his accomplishment. He basked in the pride of his people, especially his parents, but his mind kept returning to Tog. He was worried about not only this night, but the approaching winter. Chances of Tog's survival alone in a hostile environment without sufficient shelter were slim.

Monda and Auva had been concerned about their son's mysterious daily disappearances for weeks. After their huge meal of Sahndo's panther, they began questioning him more closely. Monda was curious as to how his son was able to transport this large catch alone. Auva was troubled regarding his missing fur wrap. The lake people guarded their wraps, tools and weapons almost as carefully as their fires.

He danced evasively around his parents' concerns, giving vague answers. He dismissed their worries as being baseless, stating he lost his wrap on the return trip to the village. He ex-

TALES FROM THE SUNROOM

plained that he was very close to the village when he began transporting his kill. He couldn't explain how the litter of branches was constructed when there were only scrubby bushes struggling in the rocky terrain beyond the thick green woods of the lakeshore. Sahndo stopped short of lying completely, but he remained evasive, feigning complete exhaustion so as to avoid their questions.

He spent a restless night. As soon as he heard the birds begin their morning song, he slipped silently out of the hut, filling a leather pouch with dried meat and vegetables as he left. He crept quickly to the edge of the village, through the woods, and across the plain toward Tog's hiding place. He failed to detect the figure following behind him as he hurried forward.

He was able to move more quickly as the dawn light increased, and soon arrived at the rock formation where he had left his friend. As he approached the crude but secure stone shelter, he was alarmed to discover that it was empty. Tog was gone! Panic gripped him as his eyes darted around, seeking the missing caveman. He prepared to shout his name when Tog suddenly appeared from behind a boulder, his fingers over his mouth in a signal for silence. A rush of relief surged through Sahndo, but curiosity about Tog's behavior brought him back to reality as he followed Tog's gaze. There approaching the boulders was a lone figure. They watched his progress anxiously for a few seconds before Sahndo recognized him.

He turned to Tog and whispered, "My father."

Tog quickly secluded himself behind the thick cover of the boulders, and Sahndo moved away from the area toward his father. Monda waited for Sahndo's approach, and soon the two were deep in discussion.

Sahndo was angry because Monda had followed him, and Monda was angry because he believed Sahndo was deceiving them. As their voices reverberated and echoed off the hard stone walls, Tog listened. He had no wish to hurt anyone, especially the only one who had been kind to him since he lost his family. He slowly moved from behind the rocks, exposing himself to extreme danger. Monda stopped abruptly, his eyes filled with terror as he spied Tog. He shouted a warning to Sahndo, placing himself between his son and the dreaded caveman. He pulled his large knife from the sheath at his waist, preparing to defend against the beast.

"No!" Sahndo screamed, knocking his father off balance as he wrenched the weapon from his grasp.

After a few harried moments of confusion and chaos, the small group settled down. Monda realized that Tog was no stranger to Sahndo, and Tog began to believe that maybe he wasn't going to be killed after all.

The three sat down in an uneasy circle, and Sahndo explained Tog's presence, and where he had gone each day for more than a whole moon. Monda began to comprehend his son's strange, elusive behavior even though he did not approve of it. Sahndo proposed bringing Tog into their village as a part of their family, and Monda knew the council would never accept this. Sahndo's next suggestion was even more disturbing. He would spend the winter with Tog at the pond.

At this declaration, Monda leaped angrily to his feet. Tog immediately curled into a defensive mass, his arms covering his head protectively. Once again confusion and chaos reigned until reason triumphed. After further discussion, Monda agreed to present the idea to the council, but he held no false hopes of Tog being accepted.

"I will take responsibility for Tog, " pledged Sahndo earnestly.

Monda looked at his son in surprise, which quickly turned to pride. He had grown up. And Monda had no doubt that his willful son would stick to his determination to protect this caveman. However, Monda's mind was tormented by the knowledge that Tog's kind had always been feared and hated by the lake people as dangerous, treacherous half-humans who were murderous savages.

He sighed resignedly, shook his head, and turned to go, promising to speak to the council as soon as he returned to the village.

After several hours of pleading with the unrelenting council, Sagga, a respected elder, raised his hand for silence.

"Monda's family has always been respected for their fairness and honesty. I have known both his father and grandfather. They were just, honorable men. So are Monda and Sahndo. Let some of us go out to meet this caveman and make a decision. We will take our shaman with us. She will know the spirit of this man, be it good or evil."

Soon Monda and three council members along with Silda, the shaman, were standing before Sahndo and the terrified Tog. Silda carefully studied this strange half-man, stepped forward, extended her hand to him, and smiled warmly. He slowly, shyly, hesitantly extended his finger until he gingerly touched her hand. She kindly closed her fingers and gently shook his hand.

"There is no evil in this man," she announced decisively.

They arrived back at the camp in the late afternoon. The people clustered nervously as the group entered the meeting center. An uneasy murmur arose and several mothers pulled their children to them. Just as Sagga prepared to address their fears and doubts, they were interrupted by terror stricken screams.

They turned to the source of the chilling sounds and observed Amik running from her hut, blood streaming from the side of her face.

"My mother, my mother, he's killed my mother!"

Bruel appeared behind her, cursing and screaming for her to get inside their hut. He was holding a large club in his hand, and there was blood on his clothes. As he closed on the frantic Amik, the others were frozen in shock. Suddenly one made a move. Tog stepped into the path of Bruel, causing him to stop in fearful confusion. He drew in his breath, dropped his jaw and attempted to retreat. He was a bully to the weak, but this massive man was a challenge he wasn't prepared for. As he began to retreat, the others recovered, and several restrained Bruel to prevent his escape while Silda and some of the other women hurried to see about Kesa. Auva took charge of Amik and hurried to Silda's hut with her. She could clean the wounds until Silda arrived.

Kesa was not dead, but she was badly injured. She had been rendered a heavy blow to the head, and was unconscious. Silda drilled two holes in her skull with a sharp bone so as to relieve the pressure. Kesa's right eye was fully dilated, and her right arm and leg lay motionless.

As soon as possible, Silda turned her attention to Amik. There was a large gash down her face, from the corner of her left eye to just below the corner of her lip. It was not so deep as to have caused nerve damage. It looked as if Amik pulled away just as Bruel attacked her, causing the knife to slash nearer the surface, missing her eye. There would, however, be a deep and lasting scar.

Tog was placed under the protection of Sahndo and his family since he was instrumental in preventing an even greater tragedy. Bruel was guarded all night, and early the next morning, he was escorted far across the plain to an isolated spot. He was released with a knife, his robe, a bladder of water, and one day's food rations. He cursed the group violently as they left him to his own devices.

TALES FROM THE SUNROOM

Tog's actions during the violence had won him the grudging respect of the villagers. Some were still uneasy but grateful to him for his intervention with the violent Bruel. They were relieved to be rid of him.

In two days, the hunt was to proceed. Monda and Sahndo requested permission for Tog to accompany the group. It was decided that this would be more acceptable than leaving him with the village. The women, children and elderly were nearly defenseless in case they had been wrong about the caveman.

As the group prepared to leave, Sahndo stopped them as they began placing hot coals in a mud bowl baked by the fire. They stared at him in surprise as he motioned for Tog to come forward. Tog looked around, gathered leaves and twigs, took a straight stick, and a flat wood chip.

They watched curiously, moving closer, as he worked. They gasped collectively when a thin layer of smoke rose from the leaves. Tog gently blew on the smoke while carefully moving leaves and debris onto the smoking wood chip. Suddenly, a small flame erupted, creating an audible gasp from each member of the group. They exclaimed excitedly and fearfully. This was magic such as they had never seen. They calmed down somewhat when Sahndo repeated the feat, and assured them it wasn't magic but a craft all of them could learn.

Life was much simpler on the hunt since they didn't have to protect their fire. The men were more relaxed without this added responsibility, and became more accepting of Tog. They welcomed him around their fire each night, and listened with genuine interest to his halting stories of his people. They were particularly entertained by his account of confronting the hidden Sahndo at the pond. He mocked Sahndo's desperate escape attempt, looking much like the giant crab Sahndo had resembled. The men laughed enthusiastically at the tale, while Sahndo blushed profusely. Tog slapped his friend good-naturedly on the back as Sahndo laughed at himself.

The hunters moved through the wooded pond area where Tog had lived after his family's deaths. As they did, Tog understood how fortunate he was. If Sahndo had not found him, he would now be the prey of this group instead of their companion. He shivered at the realization. His eyes met Sahndo's, and he knew that his friend held the same thoughts.

They left the woods, climbed the rocky ridge and entered the grassy plains beyond where the large herds fed. They carried wood with them so as to have a fire, as the only fuel available in the grassland was an occasional shrub.

Their third day out, they spotted vultures circling. They approached carefully, expecting to see lions or bears with a fresh kill. They might catch the predator off guard and defenseless, and make an easy capture. What they saw disturbed and frightened them. It was the mangled remains of a man. Upon closer inspection, they recognized Bruel. His fate was horrible but not surprising. He had failed to follow the major law of his people—the protection of the family—and had suffered the drastic consequences of expulsion from his village. It was an impressive, meaningful, yet difficult, lesson for them all. Especially the young.

They buried Bruel's remains, placing his belongings in with him. This was the last act of kindness they could perform for their troubled brother. They asked the Spirit God to accept this angry man, and turning, they left him there.

The hunt lasted for fourteen days. They were usually out much longer, but the herds were located early on the eighth day of the hunt. Tog was a master hunter, and they killed three buffalo in one day. They labored far into the cold night, butchering and preparing the meat for transport. Early the next morning, six of the group set out to return the provisions to the waiting village. Four carried the meat wrapped in skins, and two guarded against possible attack by predators. As they left, Tog promised Sahndo that before two more hunts, they would have horses to carry the loads. Sahndo was surprised by Tog's words, but he did not question them. He had learned to trust what his friend said. However, he had never known anyone to use a horse, and he had a nagging doubt that even Tog could accomplish such a feat.

On the fourteenth day, they saw a massive herd of caribou in the distance. They were able to kill two with their arrows before they stampeded out of range of their weapons, and at the next dawn, the remaining hunters began their six day trip back. There was light snow on the ground, so they were relieved to be going home.

The success of the hunt and the misery of the cold caused them to push harder. They stopped in the woods, built litters, loaded their bounty, and hurried forward, one carrier in front and one in the rear. They arrived back at the village late on the fourth day, making good time. The other hunters had returned five days earlier, reporting their success on the hunt as well as the death of Bruel.

In the days following the elation of a successful hunt, and the assurance of ample food for the long winter, the council met to make a decision regarding Kesa and Amik. Kesa was blind in her right eye and paralyzed on her right side as a result of Bruel's last attack. Amik had a large, red scar down her face, and it was feared no lake man would take her for a mate. It was necessary that they be protected by someone; therefore, the council decided to ask for a volunteer family to take them in. Life was difficult enough, and asking any family to take on the added responsibility of a disabled woman and her disfigured daughter was a tremendous request.

Connected

Several couples whispered together, some of them with great animation, but none came forward. Monda glanced helplessly at Auva. Their eyes met and an unspoken message crossed the space between the couple. Suddenly, there was a movement to Monda's right, and Tog stepped forward.

"I will care for them," he offered.

Shocked gasps met his offer, and uneasy murmurs rippled through the crowd. Monda waited to hear the council's response before making his own offer.

"I will be Kesa's son, Amik's brother," he continued. There was great sadness in his eyes as he gazed longingly at Amik, accepting that he was safe, but with people not of his kind, and would therefore never be completely accepted. He would probably never have a mate or sons and daughters of his own. Monda, Auva and Sahndo felt his anguish, and ached for this gentle caveman they loved.

The council clustered together, talking softly and earnestly. Sagga turned to Tog and stated, "We will let Kesa and Amik decide."

It was difficult to know how much Kesa comprehended with her brain injury, but she slowly raised her left arm and nodded her head. There were tears of gratitude, doubt, uncertainty, and resignation on her cheeks. She and Amik were completely helpless. Amik clung to her mother, and also nodded her uneasy acceptance to Tog's offer.

Monda stepped forward, stating, "My family will help also. We will move their hut beside ours, and make certain their needs are met and that they are safe."

The villagers were relieved. It was settled. Thus the heart-wrenching family was formed. Tog with his shocking appearance but gentle demeanor, Amik with her scarred face, and Kesa who was partially blinded and unable to walk or perform any

TALES FROM THE SUNROOM

duties for her village or family.

The winter passed slowly and little was seen of the unlikely kinsmen. There were, however, no angry voices or pain filled cries heard from the hut. Occasional laughter was heard by Sahndo, and his parents, as they looked in on them. The women were well cared for, safe and warm, their faces free of fear, and Tog was happy and contented.

The population was pleasantly surprised and proud at the spring thaw when the misbegotten trio emerged into the compound. Tog carried Kesa, and gently sat her down on skins spread out by the energetic and beaming Amik. They were all peaceful, looking and behaving like any other family of the village.

Before the summer ended, Tog and Amik approached Monda, hand in hand, with a wish to marry. The village rejoiced, and there was great merriment at their wedding. Sahndo was particularly proud and pleased, finding it difficult to control his emotions as the young couple pledged themselves to each other.

The following summer, Amik presented Tog with their firstborn son, Kuva. He had large hands, and what promised to be a broad chest like his father. His hair was brown like his mother's, but tightly curled like Tog's. He was immediately accepted by the whole village.

Sahndo watched his friend, his brother, holding his son as the men prepared for the fall hunt. Tog was tenderly saying goodbye to his wife and son. Sahndo marveled at the similarities of both parents in the son. As he warmly studied their happiness, it occurred to him that Tog was the last of his kind. Part of him lived in Kuva, but part was forever gone. He was being absorbed by the lake people. Tog and Sahndo would always be connected, not only by their similarities but also by their differences. The lake man wept.

He wept for Tog and his people, and also for the lake people,

Connected

his people, who had so diligently destroyed these noble men.

Tog turned, caught the eye of his friend, smiled, and moved with him to the horses tied nearby, waiting to take them on the hunt.

Beyond the Gossamer Veil

The soul dares to see what the eye cannot.

—g. gurley

Leigh sat nestled against the comfort of the giant oak on the bank of a small bubbling stream, basking in the maternal comfort she absorbed from this strong illusory trunk. The warmth of her recent experiences glowed within her, and she happily journeyed back in her memory to the delightful celebration of her first love.

Tommy Hall had been the love of her innocence, his sultry good looks exciting, yet frightening, somehow dangerous. He looked very much like Perry Como who was Leigh's mother's favorite singer. She would watch the Perry Como Show on TV with her family each Saturday night, dreamily thinking of Tommy, longing to be lost in his deep brown eyes...

Tommy lettered in basketball, baseball and football, was the captain of the football team, president of both the Beta Club and the Student Council at their local high school. He was respected by students and teachers alike. He was big man on campus, and Leigh was surprised and thrilled, as well as somewhat disbelieving, when he, as a sophomore, showed a genuine interest in her,

TALES FROM THE SUNROOM

a lowly eighth grader.

Leigh's best friend was Mary Kate Hall, double first cousin to Tommy. Leigh was intrigued by the concept of double first cousins, and Mary Kate explained that their fathers were brothers, and their mothers were sisters, thus making their children double first cousins.

Tommy walked to school and waited each morning for Leigh's bus to arrive on campus. He walked her to her classroom and would wait each afternoon in the hall, escorting her to the bus. He telephoned her each night, and they would talk endlessly.

Leigh was a petite girl with sparkling blue eyes and light auburn hair, which she wore cropped close to her head. She was strikingly attractive, owning the promise of someday becoming a beautiful woman. She was quite intelligent and exhibited a vivacious personality. She loved to laugh and would do so with great gusto and passion, evoking smiles from any within earshot of the gleeful, ringing reverberation.

One of her teachers once remarked to another as they heard the boisterous peels from Leigh in the gymnasium, "It's a good thing she's tiny, isn't it?"

Tommy was enchanted by this energetic maiden and genuinely loved her, but he found her defensiveness against his amorous advances confusing. She was not allowed to date yet, and their church parties, birthday parties, and sock hops were carefully monitored. Leigh's feelings were also amorous, especially in her daydreams, but she had been programmed that good girls were careful never to let boys go too far. She had heard whispers about "bad girls", and had no desire to be so labeled.

Tommy's life was on fast forward, and he eagerly lived each day, striving to constantly achieve and experience. It was as though he were programmed to accomplish on a pre-set and exact timetable. Leigh, on the other hand, was content to enjoy her friends, ride her bicycle alone through the countryside, lie under the shade tree in her grandmother's yard, searching for images in the clouds, or writing poetry. Her timetable was more relaxed, less urgent.

They dated several times after Leigh was 14, but the foundation of their relationship had been set, and Tommy made no aggressive demands. He realized she was not ready for the intimacy he desired, so he had no wish to hurt or frighten her. They would, however, remain soul mates, but timing for them was wrong in this dimension. Fate had written a prescription no human relationship could control, but their love would eventually transcend earthly boundaries and physical contacts.

Tommy graduated and went on to college. He was as successful in college as he had been in high school, playing football, active with the campus government, serving on the yearbook staff, and maintaining a 4.0 GPA. After college, he found an executive position with a large corporation, married Lauren Shaver from their high school, and settled down in their hometown of Salisbury. Over the next five years, they had two strong, healthy sons.

Leigh graduated, married and moved out of state. Fourteen months later, her daughter Megan was born, and Leigh's joy was complete. She was a devoted mother, focusing all her hopes, dreams and expectations on her tiny daughter. Her happiness, however, was short-lived as her young husband grew tired of the responsibilities of marriage and parenthood. He soon abandoned his small family, leaving Leigh to fend for the two of them. He refused to pay child support, stating defiantly, "I'm not paying the rest of my life for a mistake I made!"

Leigh returned home, and with the help of her loving parents, made a life and home for herself and Megan. It was extremely difficult but Leigh didn't complain. She was completely content with her beautiful daughter, and considered herself blessed and most fortunate. Life was difficult, true, but could have been much worse as they had each other, and Leigh's parents. She was a secretary for a major furniture manufacturer and was able to maintain a modest lifestyle for the two of them.

Leigh would see Tommy occasionally as she drove by his house. He always recognized her car and would wave enthusiastically. She would feel a small twinge of regret at these infrequent chance meetings, but would quickly dismiss these thoughts at the joy in her life with her daughter. Megan made any pain Leigh may have suffered in her decision to marry the wrong person insignificant and inconsequential by comparison.

Tommy was quite successful in his career and was quickly promoted to more responsible positions. He and his family moved to another city several hours away, and he and Leigh were destined never to see each other again.

Leigh married Ed Malone when Megan was eight years old, and moved to High Point with her new husband. He would be the man who gave unconditional love, complete devotion, and endless pride to and in both of them. He was a strong, kind, gentle man who spoke infrequently but eloquently, never criticizing or demanding, but supporting and inviting growth in the two he loved the most. Leigh's and Megan's accomplishments were also his to treasure. He had high self-esteem and was never threatened by their hopes, dreams, plans, and achievements. He recognized Leigh as an individual with her own goals, and took great pride in sharing those fulfillments with her. He would be her helpmate, her friend, and her devoted supporter for the rest of their lives.

On one fateful day, Leigh's mother gently informed her that Tommy had had a heart attack. He was in the Baptist Hospital in Winston Salem awaiting surgery, which was scheduled within a few days. Heart surgery was not a new technique in the '70s, but was still quite risky, and Leigh was frightened for Tommy and his family.

She mailed him a card with a note assuring him that he was in her thoughts and prayers. That was all and everything that she could do for him.

Tommy smiled softly as he read Leigh's card. He gently ran his fingers over her words, his mind warmed by the gentle memories of the pure, wholesome love they had shared as children. He loved his family, but the love he and Leigh had shared was virtuous and chaste, unblemished by the perplexity which so often accompanies life's progression. Absent from the memories of their love were the scars and bruises so many relationships incurred over time and space. They were free from anger, regret, pain or shame, and helped sustain him through his illness, surgery and subsequent recovery. He gently tucked her card away, and would refer to it again and again.

His doctors maintained close monitoring of his health as the years passed, but ten years later, his condition began to deteriorate as his heart weakened with disease that surgery and medical science could not help.

Leigh sat at the long table in the craft area of the local recreation center, waiting for her calligraphy instructor. She engaged in light conversation with the other women in the class, and soon discovered a connection with one.

Jane Miller was married to Doug Miller, an assistant chief at the High Point Police Department. Leigh remembered Doug from their high school back home. He had graduated two years ahead of her as a classmate of Tommy.

She chatted amicably with Jane, exchanging small talk and pleasantries. Jane mentioned that they had attended Doug's high school reunion in Salisbury that past spring.

TALES FROM THE SUNROOM

"How is Tommy Hall?" Leigh inquired.

"Oh, he died," Jane stated matter-of-factly. She spoke without unkindness, but with no idea of what effect her words would have on the unsuspecting and uninformed Leigh.

"What?" Leigh gasped. The shock of the news had literally taken her breath.

"Yeah, he died at Lauren's class reunion at the Sheraton last Thanksgiving."

"What happened?" Leigh struggled to maintain control of her trembling hands and overwhelming, smothering grief. Tommy had been 48 years old. Too young, too young.

"He had a heart attack, and died at the hospital right after the ambulance got him there. Lauren came to Doug's reunion this past April. She had been invited, and everyone was really glad to see her." Jane chattered aimlessly on.

She was relieved when one of the other women drew Jane's attention. She muttered a hasty excuse, and crept quietly, swiftly away to the privacy of her car. In the seclusion of her dark, cold, harbor, she wept convulsively, the sobs pulling savagely at her lungs and heart. She longed to scream out in her pain and anger, but the weeping was stealing her breath so that she had no strength for anything except to succumb to the deep agony.

After a few exhausting, intensive minutes, her tears subsided as she regained control. She was filled with a new, determined purpose. Somehow she had to contact Tommy, to tell him goodbye, to know that he was well. Her deep, abiding faith promised and assured her that he was indeed well, but she also knew that this same faith would guide her in her quest to realize her seemingly impossible mission. She had taken comfort in the knowledge that she and Tommy saw the same full moon, walked on the same earth. Now he had left her world.

Early the next day, Leigh made a long distance call to Mary

Kate, who was obviously glad to hear from the friend of her youth. She explained to Leigh that Tommy's heart had become diseased ten years after his surgery, and it was determined that further surgery would not help. The damage was inoperable, the prognosis grave.

There had been a family reunion several years later, and he had called all of his cousins, requesting that they attend. Mary Kate surmised that he wished to tell them all goodbye, as he was growing increasingly weaker.

Leigh felt a physical jolt in her chest and stomach at Mary Kate's information.

"Mary Kate," she gasped, "I got an invitation to that reunion. Was it the Coble reunion?"

"Yes it was. That was our mothers' maiden name."

"Oh, dear Lord, Mary Beth," she raised her eyes in prayerful exclamation. "I didn't know who it was. I didn't remember their maiden name. Oh, no, oh, no."

"No, Leigh, please don't. You had no way of knowing. He should have put a note inside to let you know or at least a return address. He obviously wanted to see you once more, but I guess he was afraid you or your husband would misunderstand."

"No, my Ed would never misunderstand. He loves me and trusts my completely, and I would never betray that trust. Oh, Mary Kate, I'm so sorry I didn't know. But it does give me comfort to know that he tried to reach me. I hope he knows I wasn't rejecting him."

"I'm sure he knows, Leigh. I'm sure he does."

Leigh traveled to Salisbury the following week, resolving to find Tommy's grave in the large cemetery near the drive-in theater they used to attend on their double dates with Leigh's good friend, Linda and her date. She glanced sadly at the now deserted theater as she drove past. It was being demolished, which only added to her sadness.

She located the office on the grounds, and soon had directions to Tommy's burial site. She walked uneasily to the grave, not certain what her response would be. Her eyes rested on his marker.

Thomas Lee Hall
1940-1988

She gently traced the letters with her fingers, a smile forming at the corners of her mouth.

Tommy was not here. She knew immediately that she would not find him in this place. It was quiet, peaceful and tranquil, with a lovely fountain, delightfully plump, domesticated geese waddling over the manicured carpet of grass. But Tommy was not here. He was in a great somewhere much more beautiful than this earthly spot. And she longed to find him.

Thus began the greatest adventure of her life.

Leigh had long practiced visualization, and found this to be a viable, safe instrument in controlling the stressors of a busy life in a sometime confusing, disorderly world. She neither feared nor was threatened by this experience.

She soon found herself in her familiar, dreamlike wheat field where she traveled when she visualized, surrounded by the nodding heads of heavy fruit, swaying gently, being moved by an invisible force which Leigh could not identify, but which posed no threat to her. It was a loving energy, which embraced the wheat.

She laughed gleefully, running playfully through the shafts, leaving no discernable evidence of her passage. She ran without effort or fatigue, feeling the ground's surface beneath her feet, but not impeded by its stability. She held out her hands as she

Beyond the Gossamer Veil

ran, allowing the ever present butterflies to land silently on her outstretched hands, and to flutter lightly against her cheeks and eyelashes, kissing her skin with their delicate wings.

She approached her beloved oak tree standing in the center of the field. She referred to it as her Tree of Life. This time instead of more wheat field surrounding the massive trunk, as it had always been before, there was a clear, wide lake with pristine water and a glass smooth surface. Leigh immediately thought that this must be Mother Nature's mirror. She felt no fear or surprise, heard no sound, but was beckoned into this body of water, which seemed to have a tangible life, a meaningful existence.

She stepped easily into the clearness, noting that the water covered her feet to her ankles, but there was no feeling of moisture, coldness, or discomfort. Her feet made no ripples or splashes, even as she walked. There was a warmth, a caressing round her feet. The experience transcended anything she had ever before known, and was even more astonishing than moving through her wheat field.

She waded slowly across, savoring each moment, not knowing where she was going, but having no fear or doubt about her destination. She moved on faith. Halfway across, the water still at her ankles, she stopped. It was not a fearful stop, nor was it doubtful in any way. She peered across the other half of the lake, and observed a misty shore on the other side. The mist was purest white, gentle and comforting. She was not being denied entry onto this shore, but felt compelled to return to her wheat field. She was aware of a loving space lying beyond the water, a space she was not yet prepared to enter. Somehow she knew Tommy was there.

The next time Leigh returned to her Tree of Life, she found a small, bubbling stream instead of the wide lake in her previous vision. She eagerly entered the stream, once again experiencing no wetness or discomfort. She watched with delight as the water flowed soothingly over her toes.

A path opened before her as she reached the shore. It led her over an arched bridge covering yet another stream. She marveled at the beauty of the bridge, the water and the flowers peeking up through the lush green of the creek bank.

The path steadily inclined, but there was no exertion to her legs as she climbed. She saw a lovely, picturesque cottage in the distance, and knew at once whose it was.

She slowed to study the structure. It was eloquent in its simple sturdiness and stunning beauty. It was large but unobtrusive, beautiful but non-pretentious. The windows were bright and shiny, sparkling in a light that seemed to emanate from everywhere, but with no single source. The roof was wonderfully thatched, and there was a single stone chimney from which a friendly curl of smoke escaped. The yard was completely filled with colorful, fragrant flowers being moved gently by the same invisible force present in the wheat field. There was not space for even one more plant in the gorgeous masses clustered there. The scene was tranquil and comforting, promising safety, wellness and total happiness.

As she drew nearer the cottage, her eye was drawn to the front entrance. It was a Dutch door, split in the middle, with the bottom closed, the top open. A figure stood in the opening, waiting. The figure waved a loving welcome as Leigh approached.

"Grandmother!" Leigh exclaimed joyously.

Soon she found herself in the warm embrace of her beloved ancestor. Leigh stepped back, laughing gaily, to examine this wonderful and remarkable individual whom she had missed so much.

She looked the same. Her hair twisted into the much-loved

bun, and the familiar apron embracing her waist. It was good to see her again, even though Leigh knew it would be only briefly. Her stay here could only be temporary.

After the initial rejoicing of their greeting, she was surprised by her grandmother's solemn tone.

"Why are you here, Leigh?" She was kind but firm.

"I really wanted to see you, Grandmother. And I was worried about Tommy. How is he?"

"Tommy is fine, Emily." There was an impatient edge to her voice, which Leigh had never before heard. It confused and bewildered her. She felt much like she did as a child when she was caught with her fingers in the icing on the cake. She left with an uneasiness and misgiving about her decision to come here.

She avoided visualizing for several weeks, but still felt drawn to the hallowed and celestial dimension she had discovered. She had a stubborn willfulness that lured her to realize her goal of seeking Tommy.

She arrived at the Tree of Life to discover that once again, the unscathed lake lay smoothly at her feet. She glided easily through it, the water once more undisturbed by her passage. At the shore, she noted the virtuous mist, moving lightly and silently, hiding from her view any terrain but not closing her out. She knew that there was something present which she was not yet allowed to see.

She stood in the water, absorbing her surroundings, not stepping onto the shore, when she caught sight of two figures standing in the mist to her left. She observed them for a short time, before realizing that it was Tommy and his father.

They were dressed in brilliant white clothing, their feet concealed by the mist. Or maybe they had no feet. She couldn't tell. Tommy's father stood on the right with Tommy being a full head taller.

TALES FROM THE SUNROOM

Her heart leaped with joy, and a warm smile crossed her face as she recognized him. He looked just the same as he had when they were young.

She made no sound to draw his attention, but stood motionless, watching him, absorbing his beauty and goodness. Suddenly his eyes met hers, and she was warmed by the gentle devotion and love directed toward her. He did not seem surprised by her presence, but moved smoothly to stand in front of her.

Neither spoke aloud, but emotions and feelings passed fervently between them. She drank him in with her eyes, eager to retain his memory.

She raised her right arm, and he raised his left arm at the same moment. Their hands touched in a soft, soothing salute. She had no concept of the meaning of this mysterious exchange, but felt genuinely comforted.

She turned to proceed back toward her tree, hesitated, looked back to behold him once more. He raised his hand in a farewell gesture, then disappeared into the mist.

Leigh found herself dwelling more and more on the fascination of this silent location. She became quiet, contemplative, pensive. She was not depressed, and smiled frequently, but was not present in mind and spirit much of the time. Her family became concerned about her, and mentioned it, asking if she was ill, or if anything was wrong. She quickly reassured them, dismissing their uneasiness. However, as she reflected on their worries, she decided to visit the counselor who had introduced her to visualization.

She called Tracy, explained what had been happening, and inquired if she should schedule an appointment for them to meet.

"I need to see you at once, Leigh." Tracy sounded alarmed. "Can you be here at three this afternoon?"

Leigh was amused by the uneasiness in Tracy's voice and

replied, "I'll be there, Tracy. Don't sound so worried, I feel fine. As a matter of fact, I feel happier than I have in a long time."

"Just be here at three, Leigh, and we'll talk."

Leigh arrived promptly at three o'clock, and was met immediately by Tracy, as she hurried from her office to the lobby. Her eyes studied Leigh's face, moving quickly and anxiously. Leigh was somewhat uncomfortable but still amused by Tracy's behavior.

"I have the gift of discernment, Leigh. Do you know what that is?"

"No."

"I can determine if someone is being led or influenced by an evil force, and when you explained what was going on, I was afraid that was happening to you. But I detect no evil around you. I see only good."

Leigh was relieved by the explanation, as she had felt slightly intimidated by Tracy's response to her call.

"No, I have never felt anything evil," she declared. "Just peace and serenity and unparalleled love. It's like nothing I've ever experienced before, and there was definitely nothing evil where I went. I would have been aware of it if there had been."

Tracy was obviously relieved, and they talked about Leigh's visits to the misty continuum for the next hour.

"Leigh," Tracy admonished gently, "you are aware that you don't belong there, aren't you?"

"Oh, yes, I know. Not yet anyway." She was thoughtful. Perhaps that's what she had detected in her grandmother's voice—that edge of impatience.

For several months, Leigh was content to avoid the mist. She was more satisfied, wiser, more mature in some intangible way, as well as being more reflective. She had never been immature, but now her demeanor was deeply serious, sedate, satisfied. She spent more time reading, talking with friends and family, watching sunsets, feeding the birds, and playing hide and seek, less time cleaning, fussing, rushing about. No one could know how she had been affected by this strange and mysterious life altering experience.

Finally, she could no longer resist the need to return to the hushed mist once more. She longed to verbalize her feelings to Tommy.

Upon arrival at her tree, the bubbling brook replaced the lake. She was somewhat curious but not concerned as she eagerly walked through the water, to the other side. As she stepped out of the water into the mist, there was no one there. She moved further in and was aware of a presence. Tommy stepped out of the mist to meet her.

"Why are you here, Leigh?"

She recognized the same edge of impatience and irritation in his voice as in Grandmother's.

"I just wanted to see that you're okay," Leigh whispered. His voice was melodic, the sound of it soothing.

He enveloped her tenderly in his arms, holding her close for a few precious seconds. He then stepped back from her, his hands on her shoulders, his eyes peering deeply and seriously into hers.

"I'm fine, Leigh, and you must not come here again. This place is not for you yet, and you must stay away."

She was relieved by his admonition. It was spoken with love, not anger or displeasure. But she knew that he meant it, and she knew that he spoke the truth.

She nodded her agreement, turned and left. She stepped into the creek, and attempted to catch one last glimpse of him. As she did, a large, flowing gossamer veil moved from her right, waving sensually but silently, with no rustling, as it fell behind her, closing the doorway to the mist.

Beyond the Gossamer Veil

The veil was white with the impression of being spider-web thin, but as impenetrable as iron. She could see nothing beyond its presence, and she sensed that its position was resolute and permanent, denying her entry, but doing so with gentle, yet firm, non-judgmental kindness.

Her mind returned to her Tree of Life where she nestled.

There was no regret or sadness about the events she had experienced. She had immense gratitude and deep humbleness for having been allowed to traverse this special place. She knew that she would never again fear death; however, she had no desire, nor need, to hurry this event, but she knew where she would go when the time was right. For now, she had loving people here who needed her, and many more exciting, wondrous things to do.

The Gazebo

A retreat, a refuge from the fray, where one can rest and renew the mind...

—g. gurley

John Kincaid looked up from his cluttered desk as the door to his office opened, admitting a burst of cold air, and Joe, the mailman.

"Morning, Joe, how ya doing?"

"Fine, fine, John, how are you? Mighty cold out there today. You got any coffee?" There was always coffee on a cold day, but he asked the same question anyway.

John slid his chair from under the desk, reached behind him to the coffee pot brewing on the pot-bellied stove near the center of the room, and grasped the handle with a thick cloth stationed on a small table. Joe retrieved his regular coffee cup from the windowsill, holding it out to receive the hot, black liquid.

"Gotta find another place to store my cup, John. This thing's colder than a witch's heart. This good hot coffee won't stay hot long."

John was the caretaker at the National Cemetery in Clayton, and his office was contained in a small white clapboard building near the gated entrance. A large stone wall

TALES FROM THE SUNROOM

dating back to the Civil War surrounded the compound. The grounds had once been home to a Confederate prison, and many soldiers, both Yankee and Confederate, were buried at the very back of the property. More recent graves lined the front of the complex, marked by simple white crosses, beautiful and dignified in their simplicity.

In the early 1900s, the citizens of that small town had sent a request to Washington, D. C., asking that the cemetery and prison site be preserved so as to ensure that the final resting place of war casualties not be disturbed. Congress had declared the site a National Cemetery under the protection of the National Parks Service with the directive that only military veterans and their family members would be interred there.

John Kincaid was the first director appointed to the new park, and he and his wife, Claire, had been uneasy about moving to North Carolina from their native Pennsylvania. However, it was a wonderful opportunity for John, so they dismissed their concerns and made the move nearly fifteen years earlier. Neither had ever regretted it. They were immediately embraced by the community. For days after moving into their small, brick bungalow near the cemetery, their front path was filled with well wishers bringing gifts of jams, jellies, canned beans, country ham, fresh sausage, crocheted doilies, and even a beautiful, warm, handmade quilt. They never felt like strangers, and were treated more like returning family than outsiders from the dreaded north.

Claire commented, "Now I understand what Southern Hospitality is."

John and Joe had become fast friends, and John made a point of having a pot of coffee on the stove during the winter, and a pitcher of Claire's good lemonade in the summer to share with Joe as his delivery rounds brought him to the cem-

The Gazebo

etery. His office was one of the few places in 1923 Clayton to have electricity as well as a small ice box, which kept the lemonade cold. And Claire's cloud light buttermilk biscuits were a special treat the two friends enjoyed daily.

"Any mail today?" inquired John, as he handed Joe a biscuit.

"Oh yeah, I almost forgot. You got a letter from Washington. It's from the Parks Service, so it must be your boss. Hope it's good news."

Joe smiled silently to himself. Joe always stayed around until the mail was read. He had an insatiable curiosity and loved to gossip, but was basically harmless and had never violated any confidence. Besides, there was never any information divulged to John by the Parks Service that could be construed as top secret. They were not a top secret agency involved in covert government affairs.

"Maybe it's a letter about my request for a gazebo to be built here." John guessed.

"You haven't heard about that thing yet? Shoot, that was months ago you asked about that!"

John laughed as he reminded Joe good-naturedly, "The wheels of big government turn slowly, Joe. And the post office doesn't exactly burn up the roads getting mail here either!"

The mailman was somewhat defensive to this lighthearted criticism, and blushed as his friend continued to laugh at him. Soon, however, he joined self-consciously in the fun.

"Yep, that's what it is," John continued, as he opened the envelope. "They've approved my request, and now I have to get three bids from builders. Do you have any ideas, Joe?"

"Nope, not right off hand, but I'll put the word out. What kind of structure do you have in mind?"

"It goes right over there on that knoll, overlooking the main section of the cemetery." John walked to the window and pointed.

TALES FROM THE SUNROOM

"It needs to be big so we can have bands on the Fourth of July, and dignitaries to make speeches on other special holidays. It'd also be a good place for the riflemen to stand and give the twenty-one-gun salute at funerals. We can't have benches built in there though 'cause they'd be in the way of a band, but railing would be nice. I'd kinda like for the railing to be iron. Painted white. That'd look nice with the white crosses on the graves."

The two friends stood silently, gazing across the space, each envisioning the gazebo, and the role it would play in the National Cemetery, which invoked such pride from their small city. Finally, Joe broke away to return to his biscuit and coffee.

"Gotta go, John. Looks like snow, or worse, out there, and I need to finish my deliveries. I'll keep my eyes open for a builder, but I doubt you'll get much interest before the spring. Too nasty for man or beast out there right now."

"You're right, Joe," John agreed, "but spring comes pretty quick here in North Carolina. Not like Pennsylvania. We should be able to get started on it by mid-March. And I have to get the bids in and mailed to Washington for approval before anybody can start, so I guess I'll put up signs around town and run an ad in the newspaper."

"All right," Joe drawled. "Sounds good, and I'll be happy to help put up the signs. See you tomorrow, John. Take care."

January passed and February arrived. John had gotten only one bid for the gazebo, and it was much too high. The man offered to build it for $750, which included an iron railing, but a new house could be built in 1923 for $600. Even the U. S. Government didn't have that kind of money to throw away on a project like this, so John was beginning to fear his dream of having the structure might not happen. They would accept less than three bids if less than that were entered, but John was embarrassed to send this one in. He was disappointed.

The Gazebo

He arrived at work early one cold February morning. It promised to be a sunny day as the sky was bright yellow and cloud free. He particularly enjoyed dawns in the winter, as the sun danced over icicles suspended from the eaves, and off the frosted stars on the windowpanes, turning the plain little office building into a sparkling fairy castle for a few brief moments.

As he approached his office, he spied two figures huddled on the porch by the door. They saw him coming, and stood up to greet him. It was a man who appeared to be in his early forties, and a young boy of about fourteen or fifteen. They were dressed in worn overalls, and coats with tattered cuffs, but were clean.

"Morning," John greeted them, smiling warmly.

"Morning, sir," the man responded. The youth beside him nodded his head, returning John's smile.

"Can I help you?"

"Yes sir, my son and I saw your sign wanting someone to build a gaze-bow, and we'd like to do it."

John smiled at the mispronunciation, but sensed that there was something special about these two men. Their eyes were bright and intelligent, their demeanor confident. He was suddenly relieved that they were here, and his hopes of getting the project done increased.

"Great, great," he answered enthusiastically. "Please, come on in. I'll have a fire built directly, and we can talk."

Soon the coffee was perking, and the biscuits were under the stove, warming. Strange, he thought, Claire had mistakenly made extra biscuits this morning, and packed them for me, and now these strangers are here. There's enough for them too, and they look like they could use the food.

He pulled chairs up to the stove for the two guests, and they chatted pleasantly while drinking coffee and sharing Claire's biscuits. They discussed specifications of the proposed project, and after a lengthy discussion, the older man stated, "We can do the job for $250."

John dropped the papers in his hand, and exclaimed incredulously, "Are you sure?"

"Yes sir, we can do it for that, but we can't do it for less."

"Is that with iron rails?"

"Yes sir, and we'll also put iron lattice work under the roof. We'll do a good job for you."

John was nearly hysterical with joyful disbelief, though he tried to maintain a certain decorum and dignity.

"But this is a big building. It'll have a diameter of fifteen feet. That's a lot of ironwork. Are you sure you can do it for $250?"

"Yes sir." He was smiling. "We can do it for $250."

"Well, uh, uh," John stuttered, "I'll have to have a written estimate with a sketched plan to send to my superior in Washington. It has to be approved before the contract can be given." He scrambled through the desk clutter, seeking a blank estimate form, since the two had nothing that looked like company paperwork with them.

Joe arrived as the two were preparing to leave later that morning. He stared at them curiously.

"Joe, this is Isaac Allred, and his son, Jacob. They're interested in building our gazebo." Joe couldn't help noticing John's enthusiasm, and found himself drawn into the excitement was well.

He chatted briefly with the two, learning they lived in the country, and walked here from their home. They had a blacksmith shop behind their house, and created their ironwork there.

After they left, John shook his head in disbelief at Joe. "You beat all, you know that, Joe? I was with them for several hours, and you found out more from them in two minutes than I did all morning."

The Gazebo

"You gotta ask, John. You gotta ask!"

Less than three weeks later, approval arrived from Washington. Work could begin on the project as soon as the weather permitted. It was already March 3 when the letter came, but a late February snow still blanketed the ground. Courageous crocus blooms shivered through the white crust, dotting the landscape with bright splotches of color, and the promise of a soon-to-arrive spring.

By March 25, the bright southern sun had devoured the last remnants of the recent snowstorm. Isaac and Jacob excavated the damp earth, and poured the sturdy footings, which would soon support the solid, secure foundation.

Watching the two work became a favorite pastime of the townspeople. They worked efficiently and diligently, taking few breaks and laboring from sunrise to sunset. Food was no problem as the women in town kept them well fed. John worried about their lack of transportation, but they gently rejected his invitations to stay with him and Claire when they worked particularly late. They also declined invitations from farmers to ride home in wagons or carts.

The foundation was soon completed, and the four-inch thick oak planks were spiked down as flooring. Everyone agreed that the floor alone would probably survive at least five hundred years. By the end of April, the eight-sided roof was resting on substantial wooden posts, awaiting the much anticipated ironwork.

John and Joe shared coffee and biscuits each morning with the two craftsmen on the newly constructed floor. It was amazing, but as soon as they mounted the seven steps and entered the building, a peaceful tranquility embraced them. It was impossible to be despondent or angry under the canopy of this octagonal roof. It was as if the spirit was renewed in this quiet space.

Claire and their sons, Aaron, thirteen, and Christopher,

TALES FROM THE SUNROOM

eleven, brought a picnic lunch each day to share with John, Isaac, and Jacob, along with the other food brought by the townspeople. They sensed the same restful, hushed stillness in this placid gazebo. A visit renewed and refreshed the human essence, and heightened awareness of the beauty surrounding them. The boys had romped and scampered among the lines of white crosses for all of their lives. There was no disrespect or dishonor intended, but just childish carelessness regarding the hallowed grounds. Suddenly, in this structure overlooking the grounds, they viewed the crosses much more maturely.

"I wonder who they were?" mused Aaron.

"They were fathers, brothers, sons, friends, patriots," answered Isaac. "They had hopes, dreams, expectations, and beliefs. And regardless of how those beliefs differed, they were all equal in spirit, suffering the same pains, and seeking the same redemption."

John was ever surprised at the deep, philosophical responses from this quiet, talented man. When he first arrived, he appeared to be ignorant, but there was an undefined wisdom in his words.

Others began to experience rejuvenation and revival under the shelter of the guardian structure. Soon it was becoming difficult for Isaac and Jacob to do their work, as there were so many people traversing in and out. John finally placed a barricade at the steps, urging his neighbors to stay clear so that the work could be completed.

Isaac gently admonished John for his concerns, and his impatience. "The work will be completed, John, in due time. The quietness of this space is for all to enjoy when they have a need. Where there is no time for quiet, there is no time for wisdom to grow."

The eagerly anticipated ironwork began arriving in mid-May.

The Gazebo

An audible gasp escaped the lips of all who first viewed this fine work. It was lace-like in its intricacy with vines, leaves, and flowers twisting and winding around, over and among each other. It's beauty and complexity rivaled Mother Nature's own design, but its strength and durability were unequaled among local experts. It dripped ethereally from each side of the octagonal roof. It was airy and surreal, but with unbendable angles and curves, promising to resist and deter attacks from time, weather, and mischief.

John was incredibly pleased with the masterful work, but couldn't help wondering when the two had time to complete this complex trim. Perhaps they had help at home. Lots of help.

By mid-July, the iron railing on the sides and steps had been installed. John and his family had supper in the nearly completed monument one evening after Isaac and Jacob left for the day. Reluctant to leave, the family lay on their blankets spread over the floor, listening to the rasping song of the cicadas, watching the birds fluttering busily to their nighttime roosts, and reflecting on the magic of this special refuge. The last day of work for Isaac and Jacob was to be tomorrow, and they did not plan to attend the dedication on September 1. No amount of pleading or coercing could convince them otherwise.

The small family slowly wound their way out of the cemetery toward home, as the final rays of the summer sun slipped away. The fireflies twinkled around them while John reflected on the results of the project. He was content with his role in its creation, but melancholy because he was losing two very important friends in Isaac and Jacob. He had deep affection and respect for both of them, but knew so little about either. They had focused only on their work, and spoke little of themselves. Even the persistent Joe had been unable to get any further information from them than he had on their initial meeting.

TALES FROM THE SUNROOM

Claire baked a chocolate cake to give the two, and many neighbors arrived with offerings of food the next day. There was potato salad, fried chicken, country ham, deviled eggs, and what seemed an endless bounty of delicious treats. Soon a festive, impromptu celebration of appreciation to Isaac and Jacob emerged with much laughter, feasting, and warm fellowship.

"John," Joe shouted above the laughter and voices. "Give us a speech!"

"Yeah, give us a speech!" the crowd agreed jovially.

John threw a threatening glower toward Joe as he slowly ascended the steps of the gazebo to address his friends. He was uneasy talking to large groups and had no idea of what to say. As he stood there gazing at his friends and neighbors, his eyes settled on Isaac and Jacob, and the words began to flow easily from his heart.

"Many months ago, I received permission from Washington to have a gazebo built here on this complex. I felt it was a fitting way to honor those resting here as we can sit in this open shelter, protected from the rain and the hot sun, and look out over their final resting place, reflecting on their lives and their sacrifices.

"This magnificent structure surpasses my greatest expectations and dreams, and not only allows us to honor these souls, but it also affords us a place to rest and relax and rejuvenate our own wounded spirits. On the first day that I met Isaac and Jacob Allred, I shared with them my wish for a special place for people to come and be renewed. I'll never forget what Isaac said. I can't quote him exactly, but I'll try to remember it the best I can.

"He said, 'A person may spend a whole lifetime searching for a relaxing place and not recognize it when it's found. The most difficult task is sometimes knowing what is relaxing and comforting without feeling guilty about borrowing a piece of time

The Gazebo

to do it. We would like to build such a place for you in hopes that all who find it will recognize it for the sanctuary and gift that it is, and use it without guilt.'"

John's eyes sparkled with emotion as he continued. "They have succeeded in building such a sanctuary, and there are no words to thank them for the lavishness of the gift they have given my family and this city. Isaac, Jacob, please come up here and accept our gratitude."

The two stood beside John and accepted the adulations of the crowd. Isaac smiled, embraced John and turned to the crowd. They became silent as he addressed them.

"It has been our pleasure to serve you good people, and we hope for you much success and joy in your lives here in Clayton. We are proud to have been a small part in the creation of this tribute to your fallen sons. However, none of us really finishes any meaningful thing in this life. We merely start it for others to continue, and we pray that you will continue to seek out the comfort and growth offered within this enclosure, and within the friendships of your neighbors, the love of your families. We draw our strength from each other, not a structure."

Later John sadly watched the two as they left. Somehow he knew he'd never see them again. For all their goodness and talent, there was a mysterious air about them. No one had been able to penetrate the invisible, silent barrier surrounding them. Jacob had spoken little and infrequently, usually only to Isaac. And Isaac had been a paradox. He appeared to be uneducated, yet spoke eloquently and intelligently with a great deal of insight and wisdom. No one was able to learn where they lived or where they came from, or if there was anyone else in the family. In spite of all the vagueness, the whole town had loved these two unknown strangers. And John knew that he would always miss and remember them.

TALES FROM THE SUNROOM

The gazebo became instantly popular at the National Cemetery. Each person stepping into the space was aware of inexplicable peace and comfort. Shyness, anger, doubt or uncertainty disappeared. Bands performing there did so with perfect harmony, their instruments in constant tune. Singers were right on key with exact pitch. Speakers were confident and notable, greatly inspiring their audiences. Families visiting there found accord; bickering and arguing replaced by the joy of being and belonging together. The power radiating was undeniable, and those who remembered the builders were convinced that they were the reason for this power.

A small, bedraggled family of four children and a weary looking father arrived at the gazebo one fall day. Their clothes were worn and faded castaways, the sleeves on the only boy, too short. Their shoes were scuffed and ill fitting, but the cardboard inside to protect against the holes in the bottoms was invisible to any observer. The eight-year-old boy was grateful for this fact, as it allowed him some semblance of dignity. He was painfully aware of their rag tag appearances, and found it humiliating. He felt that everyone was staring at them with pity, and worse, contempt.

Their mother had died the year before, leaving their father to provide for them as best he could. The eleven-year-old girl did as much as she was able to care for the other three, and a woman came in daily to cook and clean. There was little left from the meager cotton mill wages of the father to buy proper clothing for his children. Their schoolteachers collected clothes for them, which were usually worn out by the time they were discarded, but the father was grateful for their efforts and concern.

The children, however, were too young to grasp the gravity of the situation, and knew only shame when others laughed and pointed at them when they wore a dress or shirt once

The Gazebo

owned by a classmate. First their mother had died, and now they were being further injured by insensitive peers. It was difficult for them to understand what they had done to deserve this. The guilt and anger at imagined misdeeds pressed them into despair and hopelessness.

They offered no objection when their father suggested they go to the gazebo at the National Cemetery, but neither did they show enthusiasm at the prospect. They had not seen this place even though it had been completed for several years. Circumstances had kept them confined to their home, the classroom, and an occasional visit to Sunday School. They had all the appearances and demeanors of prisoners of war, and their father was desperate to help his stricken children.

The youngsters walked aimlessly through the lines of white crosses, touching the tops nonchalantly, kicking at invisible rocks in the grass. The boy looked up, and caught sight of the gazebo. He moved toward it, never lowering his eyes as he approached. His sisters and father noticed his motion, followed his gaze, and fell in behind him as he reached his destination.

By the time they stepped onto the strong oak floor, their depression had lifted. Soon they were laughing and swinging on the rails and posts, the father standing nearby, happily watching, with the same sensation of lightness. It was as though a heavy weight had been removed from his shoulders, and he was once again able to hold up his head. He reached into the bag he was carrying, and pulled out the box camera he had given his wife on their last Christmas together. He snapped a picture of the happy quartet, the girls standing demurely, but smiling, on the steps, and his son standing on the bottom of the railing, leaning over with a wide grin on his face, his arm raised in a self-assured greeting. There was no embarrassment or humiliation about the too short sleeves or frayed cuffs, just the joy of life and play and being with family.

The picture was developed and framed. It set on a table in the hallway near the front door of their home as a reminder that no matter how difficult life became, there was still love and laughter and hope.

John placed a small marble marker at the base of the gazebo foundation on the day he retired from service at the cemetery. It read simply:

Lovingly erected in 1923 by
Isaac and Jacob Allred
Angels do walk among men